Sam Tuttle's

PICTURE BOOK
of OLD MASSACHUSETTS

BY SAM TUTTLE
DESIGNED BY GRETCHEN BRADLEY
AMERICANA REVIEW • SCOTIA, NEW YORK

BOOKS BY SAM TUTTLE / JOHN E. DUNCAN

Picture Book of Old Massachusetts
Picture Book of Old Connecticut
The Sea Chain
Fun and Games of Long Ago
Rascals and Rogues of Long Ago
Bikes and Trikes of Long Ago
Nostalgia Crossword Puzzles (with Nellie Meyer)

Copyright © 1992 by John E. Duncan

Published in the United States of America
by Americana Review, 10 Socha Lane, Scotia, NY 12302

Library of Congress Cataloging in Publication Data

Tuttle, Sam, 1914-
Sam Tuttle's Picture Book of Old Massachusetts / by Sam Tuttle.

Includes bibliographical references and index.
1. Massachusetts — Pictorial works.
2. Massachusetts — History — Pictorial works.
3. Engraving, American — Massachusetts.
I. Title.   II. Title: Picture Book of Old Massachusetts.
F65.T88 1992   974.4—dc20   91-46064
ISBN 0-914166-24-7

To Barbara, Deborah, and David

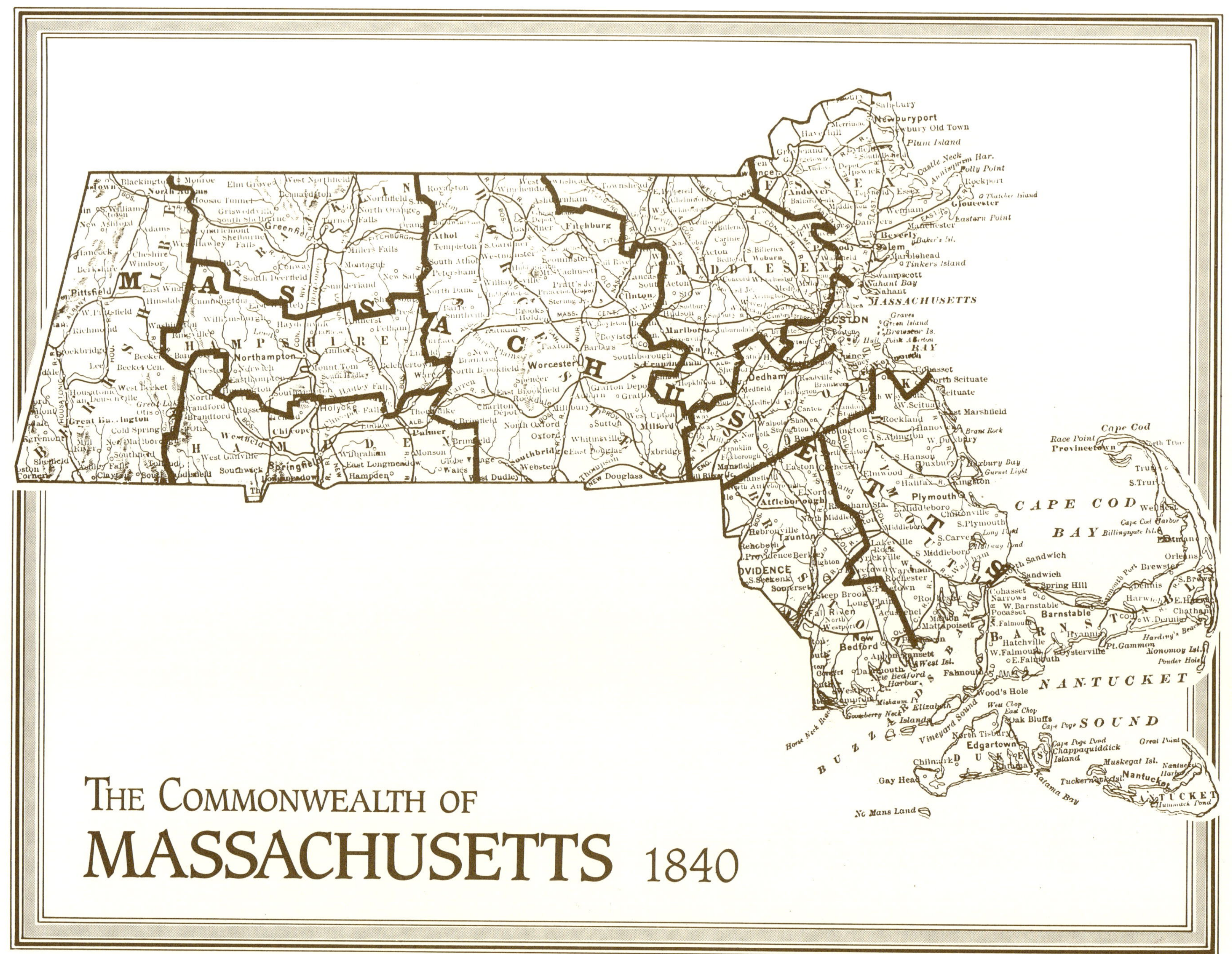

THE COMMONWEALTH OF
MASSACHUSETTS 1840

Contents

Introduction

A few words about this book and the fine Commonwealth of Massachusetts

Writing about Massachusetts in 1839, John Hayward noted that ''this commonwealth (was) the mother of New England colonies of free states, and of American liberty. The history of the state is interwoven with every political and moral event of important occurrence in the settlement and progress of the whole of North America which preceded or was connected with the Revolution of 1775.''

In that same year, John Warner Barber, whose writings and illustrations appear within these pages, observed that ''Massachusetts has ever been one of the most distinguished members of the American confederacy. The spirit of her institutions has been transformed into many of her sister states, and she may justly claim an elevated rank among the members of the United States.''

These remarks suggest a fine merging of opinion, proper pride, and facts, and if some of that respectful view has rubbed off on your author, it could happen easily, since some of my ancestors were pioneers in Rowley, Newbury, and Lancaster, others discovered the beauty of Northfield, and more recently others recognize the assets of Winchester and Newburyport.

Mild subjectivity or not, the research for ''Picture Book of Old Massachusetts'' has brought to me a fresh appreciation of the 18th and 19th century men and women of the Bay State, and of their strengths in inventiveness, industry, statesmanship, and literature, and a reminder of the diverse beauty of the state.

In this work, we use only old wood and steel engravings to show where people lived, worked, played, and worshipped, largely in the 1800's, brushing the earlier years now and then, and never touching the 20th century, where many texts already exist. We have tried to be as accurate as possible, while avoiding the threat of excessive scholarship. The little snippets dare to suggest that reading about history can be fun.

Happy reading about the great Commonwealth of Massachusetts!

Sam Tuttle

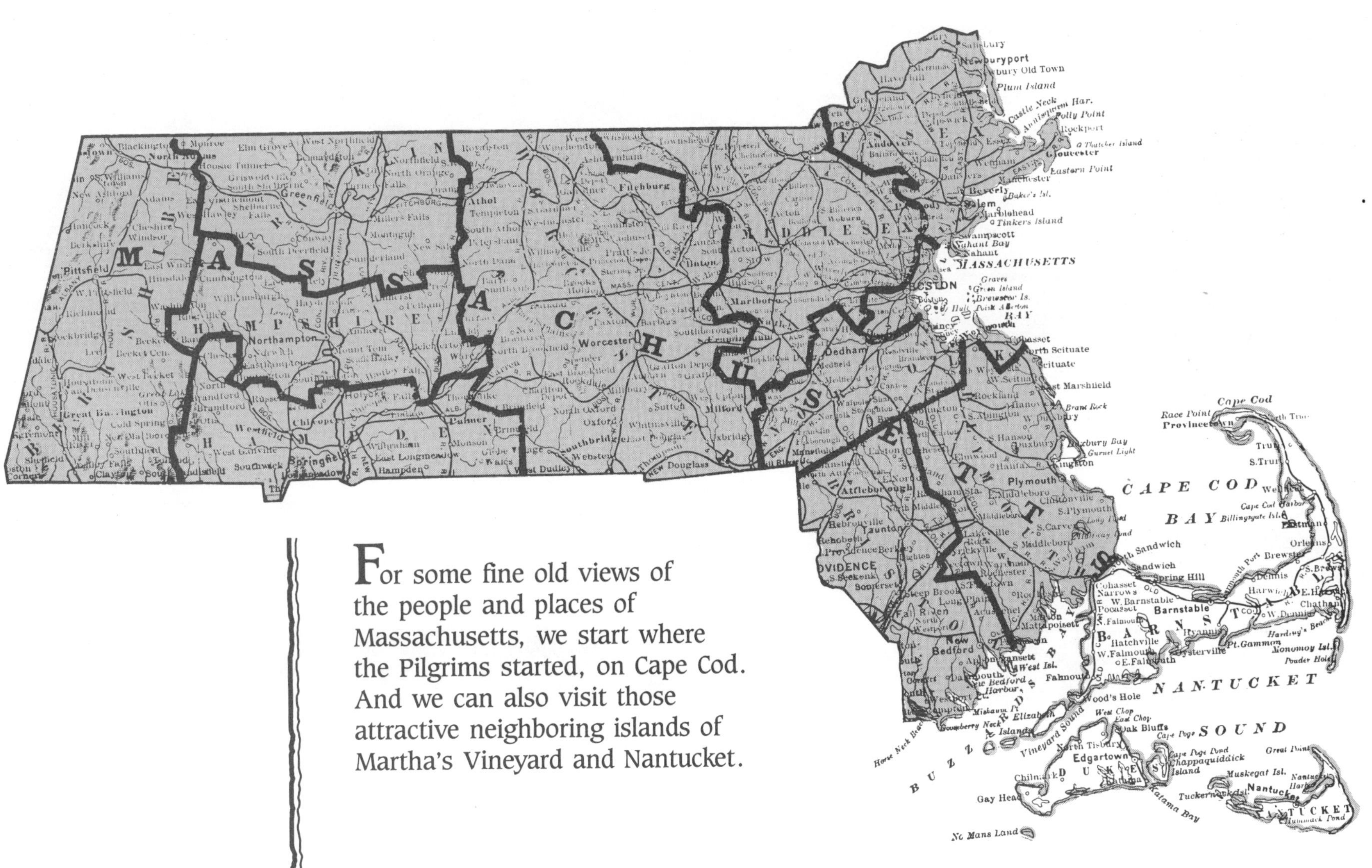

For some fine old views of the people and places of Massachusetts, we start where the Pilgrims started, on Cape Cod. And we can also visit those attractive neighboring islands of Martha's Vineyard and Nantucket.

BARNSTABLE, DUKES & NANTUCKET

COUNTIES

The Mayflower

Fifty-three days after sailing from Plymouth, England, the 108-foot long Mayflower anchored in Provincetown harbor, at the tip of Cape Cod. This sketch was drawn in 1839, when the town population was nearly 2,000.

The illustrator for William Cullen Bryant's account of the landing shows many of the 102 courageous passengers of the Plymouth company. Bryant explains that woods of oak, pine, ash and walnut were found at that time, but eventually gave way to the shifting hills of yellow sand.

One Mayflower passenger, in describing the Provincetown scene, observed that "one thousand ships may safely ride in this harbor. Every day we saw whales playing hard by us…if we had the means to take them, we might have made a very rich return." This view of the village was sketched in the 1800's.

The Highland Light at North Truro saved many a ship and crew, but could not protect the seaman from all of the dangers of the sea. In the great gale of 1841, some fifty-seven men from Truro were lost at sea. The early name for Truro was Dangerfield.

The central wharf at Provincetown, where the local seamen unloaded their catches of cod and mackerel. In describing the fishermen, one writer said simply that "their home is the ocean."

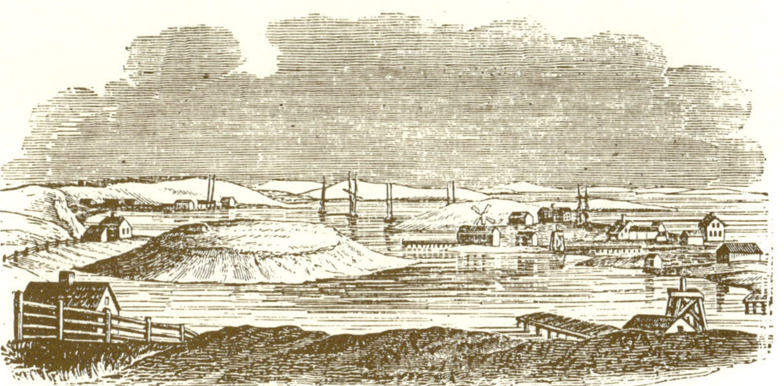

Wellfleet, on the west side of the Cape, was well known for its substantial fishing industry. John W. Barber, who sketched this view of the harbor, cited its further claim to fame: in 1797 thirty pairs of twins were born here, plus two sets of triplets.

Brewster, shown here, was a major center of salt production in the mid-eighteenth century, and a popular retirement center for many sea captains.

As late as 1839, it was claimed that this pear tree at Eastham was two hundred years old, and vigorous. The town was one of many communities served by the Old Colony Railroad. Nearby Orleans' shores provided clam diggers abundant rewards. In 1802, one historian noted that 1,000 barrels had been collected, and a man could earn seventy cents a day for his labor.

Chatham, at the southeast angle of the Cape, was called Monomoy by the Indians. Incorporated in 1712, it claimed a large cranberry crop from that area, and by 1870 had 380 employees working in several fisheries.

At Yarmouth, shown here, and at Dennis and several other towns on the Cape, salt making was a major source of jobs and income during the 19th century. In the single year of 1837, Yarmouth had 52 salt-making establishments, producing 365,000 bushels.

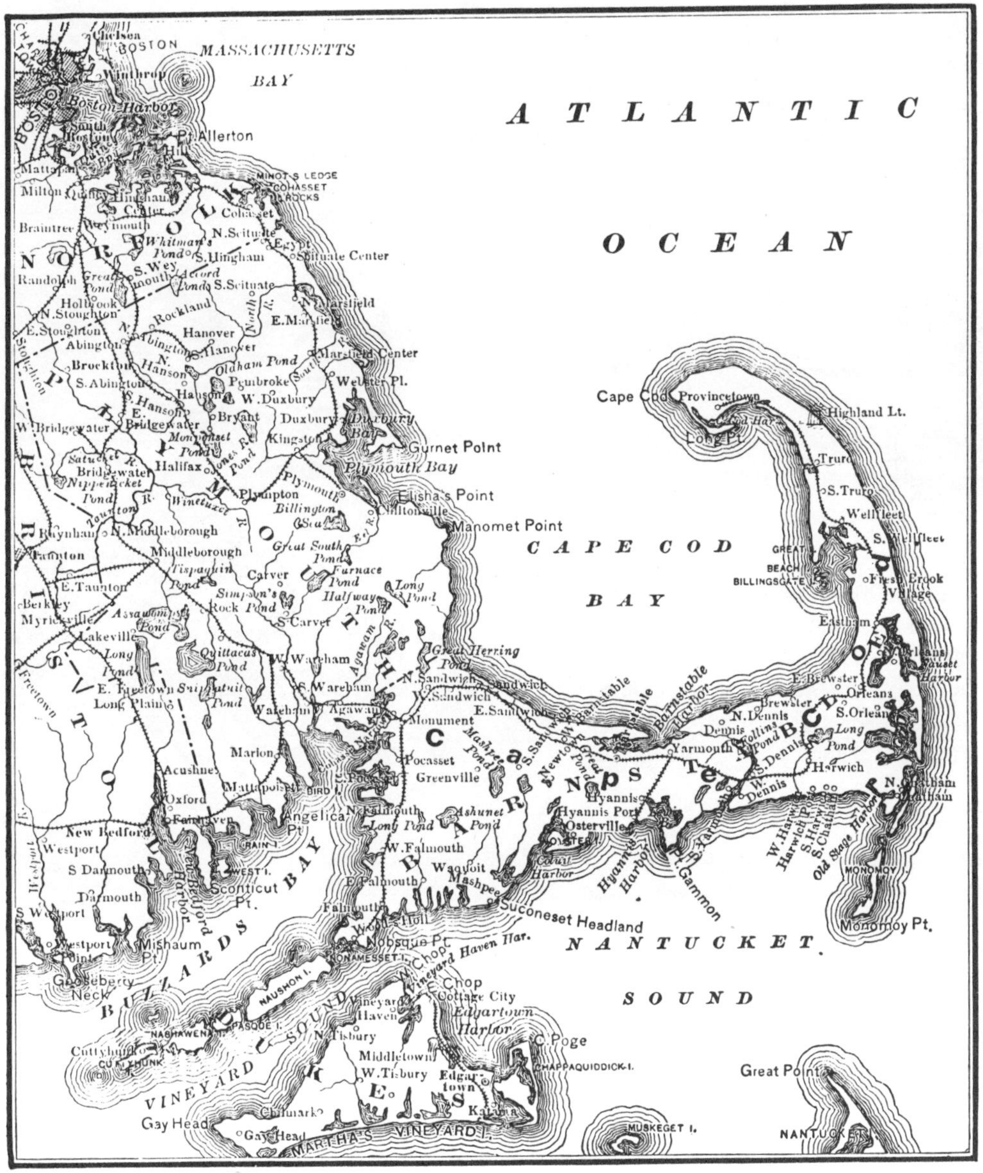

Mashpee, once known as Marshpee, was named for the Indian tribe living in that area of the Cape. This sketch shows the old Indian church near that town, still standing.

Century magazine in 1883 featured this map of Cape Cod and the adjoining areas from Plymouth to Boston. The Old Colony Railroad appears on the Cape, but no roadways. Martha's Vineyard appears at the bottom, and a part of Nantucket.

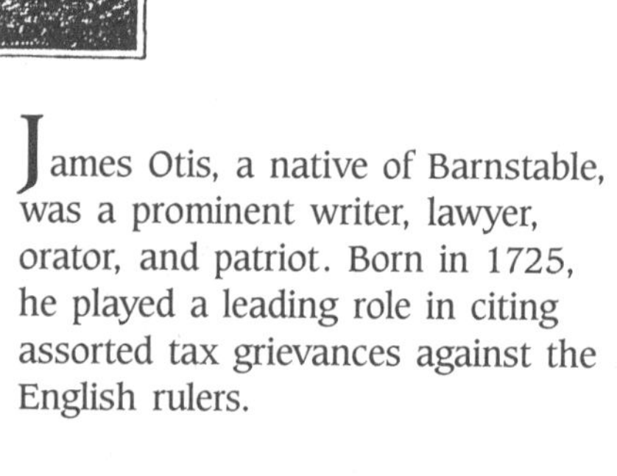

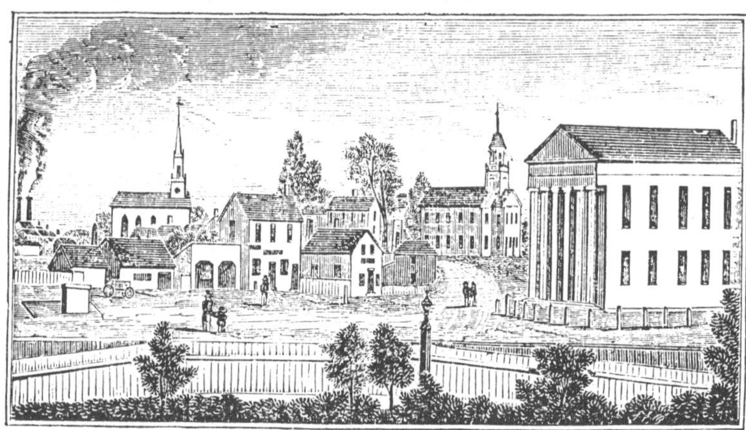

Barnstable in the 1800's was already a thriving village, township, and county. The courthouse is shown at the right. Salt was made here as early as 1779, selling for $6 a bushel.

James Otis, a native of Barnstable, was a prominent writer, lawyer, orator, and patriot. Born in 1725, he played a leading role in citing assorted tax grievances against the English rulers.

Dr. Timothy Dwight, the eminent New England theologian, traveler and writer, called them simply "Cape Cod houses: one story, four rooms on the lower floor, 18-inch pine shingles on both sides and roof, chimney in the middle, and two windows on each side of the door." The name and style remain.

The village of Sandwich was settled in 1637, and by 1840 had more than a hundred homes, a nail factory, and a glass factory employing one hundred hands. The township of the same name counted a population of 3,600. Its attractiveness remains.

Osterville, between Hyannis and Cotuit, shared with those towns a steady growth in the tourist trade in the 19th century. Pictured is the Cotocheeset House.

Falmouth was founded by the Quakers in 1661. For many years it prospered from its substantial whaling trade. This sketch of the village shows the road to the southwest, where Wood's Hole sailboats ferried the mail three times a week to Martha's Vineyard, in the 1840's.

Through much of the 19th century, Hyannis received notice only as a small area of the town of Barnstable, "near the entrance to Lewis Bay, near Yarmouth." By 1839, Hyannis had two churches, as well as a good harbor and a new federal government breakwater under construction.

The Cape Cod Ship Canal.

The long talked of ship canal across the peninsula of Cape Cod, Mass., has been surveyed, and preparations are making for the immediate prosecution of the material part of the work. The canal will be about eight miles long and without locks. It will connect Cape Cod Bay with Buzzard's Bay, and not only shorten the water route between New York and Boston by 90 miles, but will secure an in shore route between these cities practicable for such passenger and freight boats as now ply on Long Island Sound.

An 1880 news item from the Scientific American gave notice that construction of the Cape Cod canal might soon proceed. This was of considerable interest to the shipping trade, and to such area towns as Falmouth, Bourne, and Wood's Hole. Actual building of the canal began twenty-nine years later, in 1909, and work was completed in 1914.

Edgartown, shown here, is joined to Chappaquiddick Island by a small bridge. The two islands make up Dukes county.

A handsome side-wheeler approaches Martha's Vineyard. The island was discovered by English explorer Bartholomew Gosnold in 1602. He wanted to start a settlement there, but his crew wanted to return to England, and they prevailed. Both Martha's Vineyard and Nantucket were originally claimed by New York, but were annexed by Massachusetts in 1692.

An old house at Edgartown, on Martha's Vineyard. In the 1800's, woolen blankets, socks, and mittens were made and sold here, and many friendly Indians lived on the island in the seventeenth century.

Bachelder's guide to popular resorts of 1876 describes the excitement as the steamship approaches the rural city of Oak Bluffs, ''where rises a colossal structure surrounded by broad verandas and towering cupolas — The Sea View House.'' This is it, and Mr. Bachelder says that 69,000 guests visited this renowned resort in 1874.

The Nantucket wharf was bubbling with activity long before the advent of the 20th century, whether the visitors were seeking quiet and repose, seaside sports, fine hotels and boarding houses, or attending meetings and lectures.

John W. Barber sketched this view of the town of Nantucket from the inner harbor in 1839. The town, the island, and the county share the same name. It was sold to Thomas Mayhew and some of his friends in 1660 by the two Indian sachems of Nantucket for thirty pounds and two beaver hats.

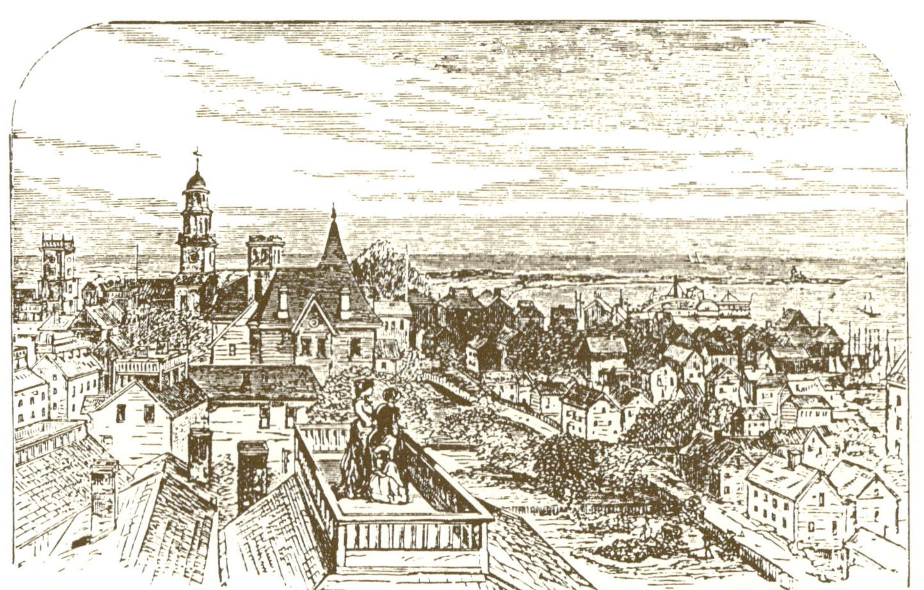

Nantucket from its house-tops, about 1850.
From these railed platforms, the dwellers might
sit in the cool of the evening, taking note of
the passing ships.

A few miles from Nantucket lies the sleepy
village of Siasconset, the fishermen outside
their modest huts in this old drawing. Whaling
on Nantucket began about 1690, and as late as
1837 the island employed 74 vessels in a whale
fishery; and more than a million gallons of
whale and sperm oil was imported, with huge
sales of oil and candles.

12

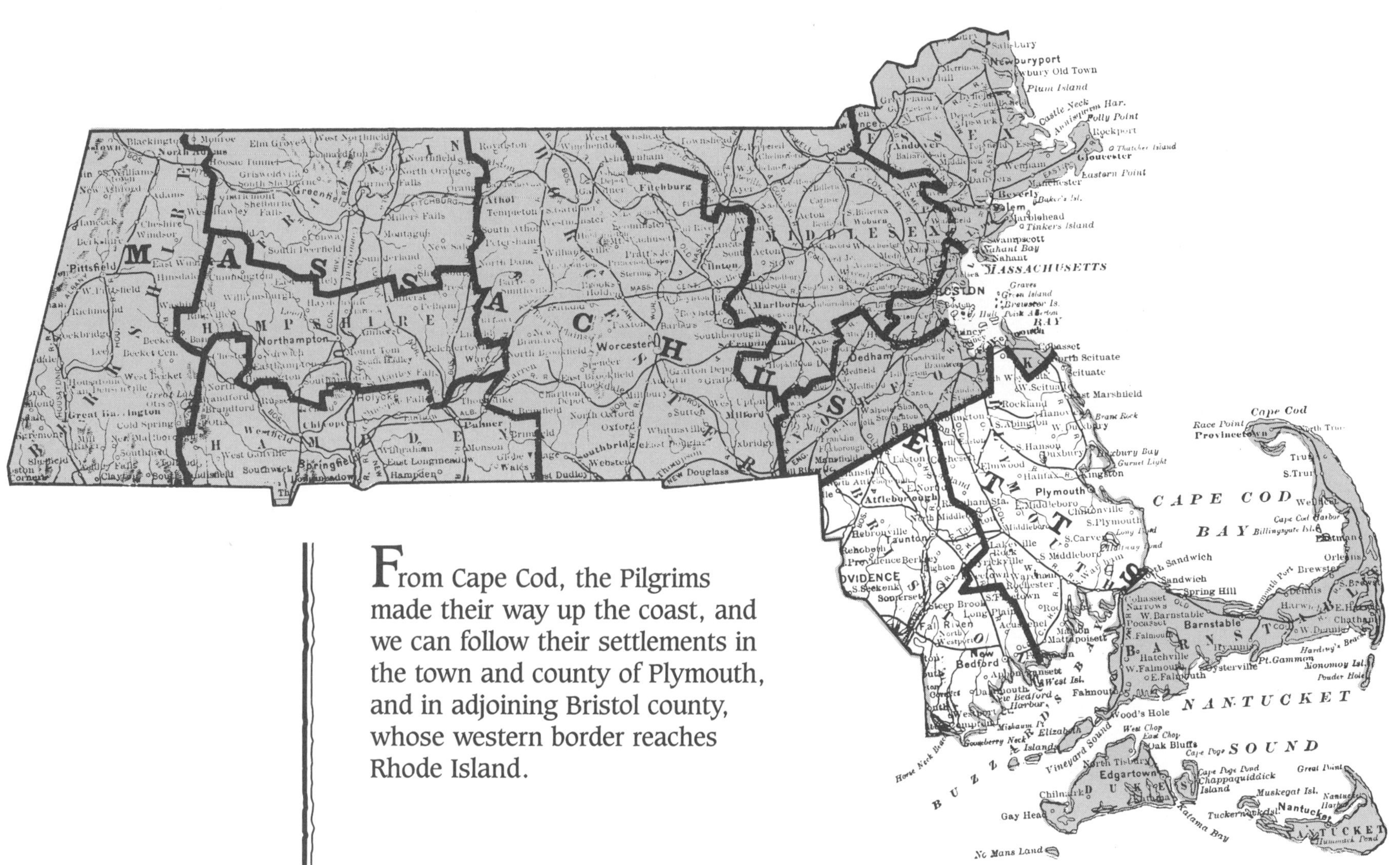

From Cape Cod, the Pilgrims made their way up the coast, and we can follow their settlements in the town and county of Plymouth, and in adjoining Bristol county, whose western border reaches Rhode Island.

PLYMOUTH & BRISTOL

COUNTIES

Several weeks after their initial landing at Provincetown, the Pilgrims landed at Clark's Island, and finally at Plymouth, as depicted in these old engravings. In the larger drawing, John Alden and Mary Chilton prepare to step on Plymouth Rock. Alden was one of the leaders of the group, under Captain Miles (or Myles) Standish.

Burial Hill, above Plymouth Harbor, is a poignant reminder of the toll of the Pilgrims in their first winter. Beset by bitter cold, poor nutrition and disease, they lost all but forty-two of the one hundred two men, women and children who had arrived on our shores.

Public worship by the Pilgrims at Plymouth. The Mayflower Compact, signed by the men of the Mayflower before the landing, was a remarkable constitutional document. They had sought this new land to escape poverty and find greater religious freedom.

This view suggests the kitchen of John Alden's home as it was in 1788. Alden and Miles Standish played vital roles in establishing friendly relationships with the Indians, and together founded the town of Duxbury.

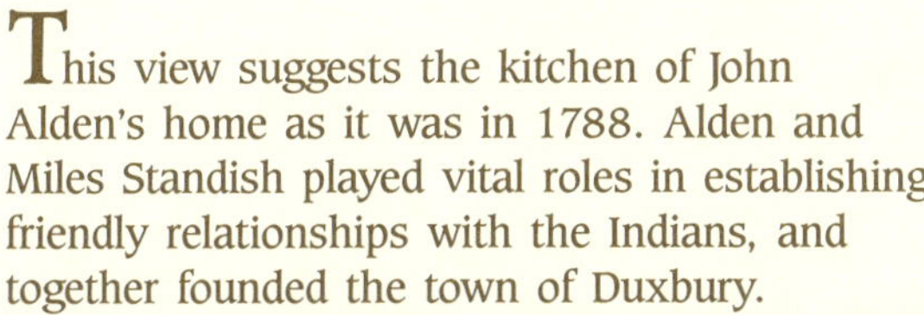

In this 19th century map of Plymouth Harbor, we can also see Clark's Island and the adjoining towns of Kingston and Duxbury. One historian, in citing the importance of the Plymouth settlement, noted that "here the right of suffrage was imparted to every citizen not disqualified by poverty or vice."

J.W. Barber's sketch of Plymouth Harbor, circa 1839, shows several church spires and burial hill in the background. The Indians called the town Patuxet.

The town of Kingston, just north of Plymouth, was incorporated in 1726. In the mid-1800's, it claimed nineteen fishing vessels, a cotton mill, nail factory, and a population of 1,371 hearty people.

Standish was a man of great courage and integrity. Two centuries after the death of Standish, a poem by Longfellow created the Standish courtship of Priscilla Mullins, who married not Standish, but John Alden.

The monument to Miles Standish at Duxbury, from an old copy of Harper's Magazine. An anniversary repast to commemorate the Pilgrim landing was started on December 22, 1769. The menu: A dish each of Indian whortleberry pudding, sauquetash, clams, oysters, codfish, sea fowl, haunch of venison, frost-fish, eels, apple pie, and cranberry tarts and cheese.

Marshfield, some 25 miles south of Boston, gained fame as the home of Daniel Webster. The great statesman, lawyer, and orator was born in New Hampshire and graduated from Dartmouth, but as his reputation grew, he moved to Boston and Marshfield, and he represented the Bay State in Congress.

The attractive Webster home at Marshfield was an elegant showpiece, but later burned to the ground.

Called Namasket by the Indians, Middleborough was incorporated in 1660. In the 1800's, it could boast two cotton mills, two forges, a nail factory, and other plants turning out shovels, spades, leather goods, tacks, and straw bonnets.

Hingham's Rose Standish House was a popular inn in the 1880's. The town offered several fine hotels, regular steamboat service to Boston, and at that time factories turning out steam buckets, umbrellas, harnesses and hatchets.

North Bridgewater was incorporated in 1821, some eighteen years before this sketch by Mr. Barber. With rapid growth, the town's manufactories were turning out more than a million pairs of boots and shoes by 1865, and had grown to 8,000 people by 1870. In 1874, its name was changed, and since that time this fine city has been known as Brockton.

Bridgewater was severely damaged by an Indian raid in 1676. During the Revolution, a factory which turned out cannon and small arms operated here. By 1840, Indian raids and armaments had given way to important educational matters, as indicated by a new state normal school, shown here.

Bridgewater was the home of the Bridgewater Iron Manufacturing Company. Among their major projects was the making of forgings for the "Monitor."

New Bedford, called Acushnet by the Indians, earned its rich history as a great whaling port, and hence a leading city of Bristol county. In 1853 there were 410 whaling vessels in the New Bedford area, importing more than 45,000 barrels of sperm oil that year.

An old whaler at anchor at a New Bedford wharf. In 1874, historian Elias Nason reported that the city was delightful, with many scenes of beauty, and a growing population of 21,000.

Frederick Douglass, the eloquent orator, upon escaping from slavery, worked three years as a stevedore in New Bedford. Receiving the respect and admiration of William Lloyd Garrison, Douglass became a leading figure in the anti-slavery fight in New England.

For much of the 19th century, Fairhaven, across the Acushnet River from New Bedford, shared the whaling activities with New Bedford. The town also produced cotton goods, leather goods, tinware and chairs.

The Fall River Line provided daily steamship service between Boston and New York, operated by the Old Colony Steamboat Company. The city was also served by several railroad lines.

Not evident in this placid view of Fall River were the signs of a town bustling with activity. In the mid-eighteenth century, Fall River manufactories turned out everything from calico clothing to iron castings and chairs, in addition to the large fishing industry. Fall River was originally called Troy.

Back in 1804, Jedidiah Morse told readers of his geography that Attleborough was thirty-six miles from Boston, and a mere nine miles from Providence, and contained 2,480 ''souls.'' Famous for its manufacture of jewelry, the township embraced North Attleborough, South Attleborough, and Attleborough Falls. These villages also produced combs, clocks, and calico.

From Boston's City Directory of 1868, our attention is drawn to the virtues of Taunton's City Hotel, one of several inns in the growing city.

SNIPPET

Fall River was the home of Lizzie Borden, 1860-1927. She was acquitted of the ax murder of her mother and stepfather, but the famous rhyme about her has survived all of these years.

22

The town of Taunton was incorporated in 1639, and incorporated as a city in 1860. This view of the Taunton Green was sketched by J.W. Barber in 1839. The city, said one historian, offered great opportunities for rest and recreation, while Rev. Nason noted that the State Lunatic Asylum ''is a splendid building.''

Praise of the architecture of Taunton's Unitarian Church came from one historian of the 1800's. There was considerable diversity in the faiths available to the loyal churchgoer, and fourteen different buildings to serve these needs.

Taunton's largest employer in the 1830's was Field's Tack factory, which could grind out nine tons of tacks or nails per day. Other plants in Taunton produced railroad cars, screws, shovels, soap, clothing, and tinware.

SNIPPET

In 1875, a typical Bay State father earned $760 a year, with $132 going for rent, $100 for meat and fish, $356 for other groceries, $76 for clothing (including shoes), $20 for dry goods, $10 for religion, $37 for fuel, $29 for everything else. The State Bureau of Statistics also reported that in many cases the fathers depended upon their children for one fourth of the total family income, while earnings by wives were so small that the family would save more when the wives stayed home.

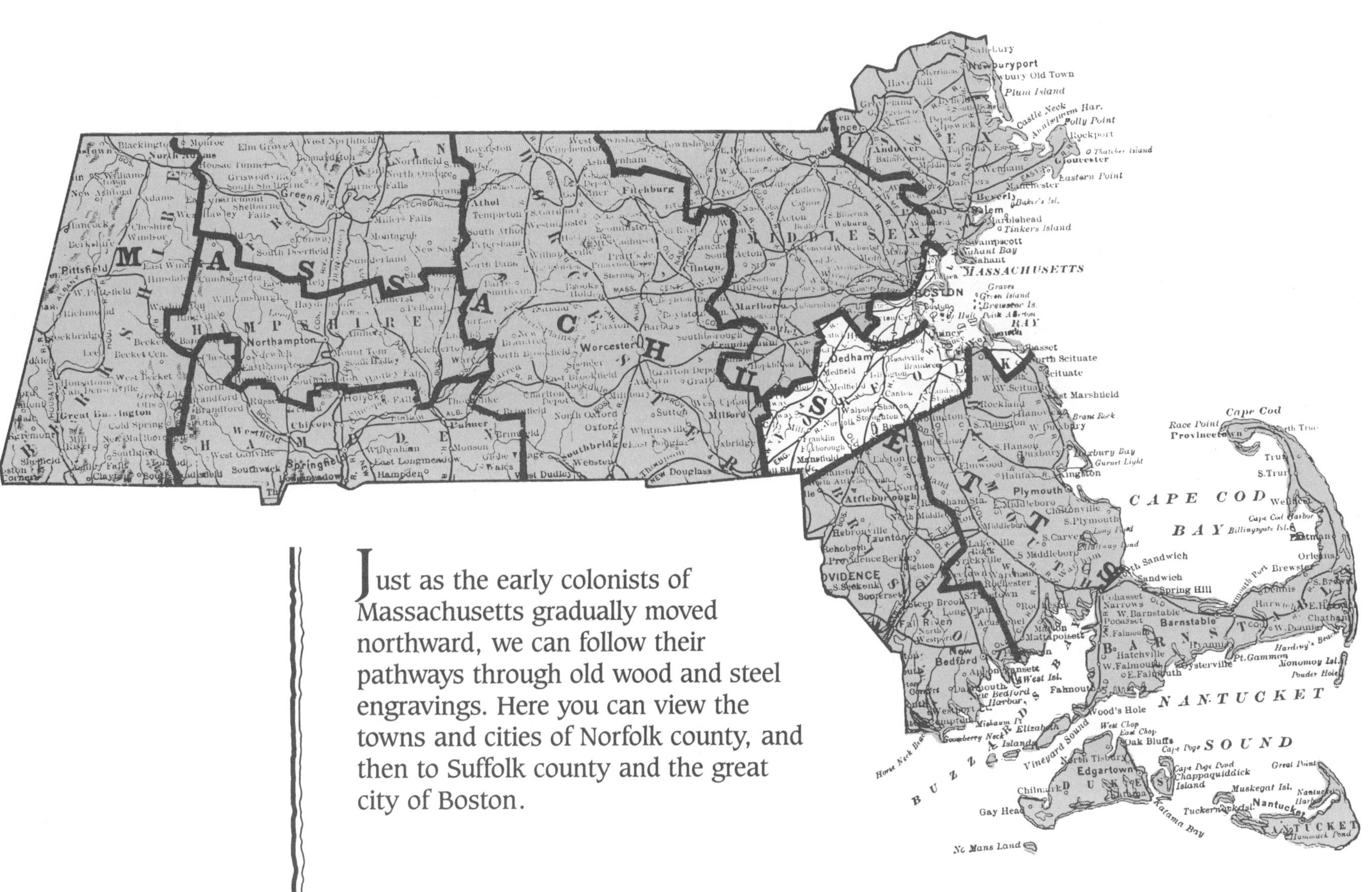

Just as the early colonists of Massachusetts gradually moved northward, we can follow their pathways through old wood and steel engravings. Here you can view the towns and cities of Norfolk county, and then to Suffolk county and the great city of Boston.

NORFOLK & SUFFOLK
C O U N T I E S

This is the harbor at Cohasset, at the eastern end of Norfolk county, on Massachusetts Bay. Cohasset was often identified by its rocky coast and numerous shipwrecks, but by the 1830's, the town also earned a reputation as a summer resort, with fine scenery and exhilarating air.

The Winthrop Church at Holbrook won special praise for its 19th century architecture, while Mr. Nason, a writer/minister of that era, described the Holbrook citizens as ''temperate, intelligent, and industrious. Everybody minds his own business, and everybody has some business to mind.'' For many residents, their business was making boots and shoes.

Back in 1622, a group of fifty men from England settled here at Weymouth, but not without problems of disease, disorder, and bad relationships with the Indians. Nonetheless, by the time this 1839 sketch was made, Weymouth had not only survived, but could boast about good roads and wonderful cheese products.

Quincy, a part of Braintree until 1792, is the birthplace of several famous Americans, notably John Hancock (shown here), John Adams, and John Quincy Adams. Hancock was a member of the Continental Congress, the first signer of the Declaration of Independence, and the first Governor of Massachusetts.

The Adams mansion in Quincy was home for members of the family from 1788 to 1927 — a landmark in this city.

Some members of the family maintained other homes in the Quincy area. This, for example, is the John Adams home, as sketched in 1893. Adams served as a two-term vice-president under Washington, before his election as president.

John Adams, as drawn by Gilbert Stuart. Although a man of brilliance and integrity, his diplomatic differences with Alexander Hamilton denied him a second term as President.

This engraving of Abigail Adams, wife of our second president, was also made from a painting by Gilbert Stuart. Abigail was a native of nearby Weymouth, and a prominent, capable person in her own right.

The senior John Adams lived long enough to see his son, John Q. Adams, (shown here) elected as the sixth President of the United States. John Quincy's son Charles Francis Adams had a distinguished career as minister to Great Britain during the Civil War years, adding further lustre to the family name.

Louisa Catherine Adams

Louisa Catherine Adams was the strong partner of John Q. Adams. She came from Boston, and joined John Q. in Quincy and the White House.

The Quincy Patriot featured a quarry on its masthead, Quincy having established a considerable reputation for its fine granite. This 1892 edition featured a front-page account of the benefits of bicycle riding.

The town of Randolph, like Quincy, was part of Braintree until 1792. Jedidiah Morse reported in 1804 that most of Randolph's 1,021 inhabitants were farmers, although some of its men and women worked in a local shoe factory.

In 1804, the people of Sharon seemed to typify the enterprise of the people of Norfolk county and of the state of Massachusetts. In Sharon, the men and women turned out axes, bedsteads, straw bonnets, leather, cotton and woolen goods.

SNIPPET

In the late 1800's, a writer noted that the people of Stoughton were turning out boots by the millions, adding that "the people are too busy to trouble each other, and too well off to move away. . . .a thriving town, with their elements of peace, health, and competence."

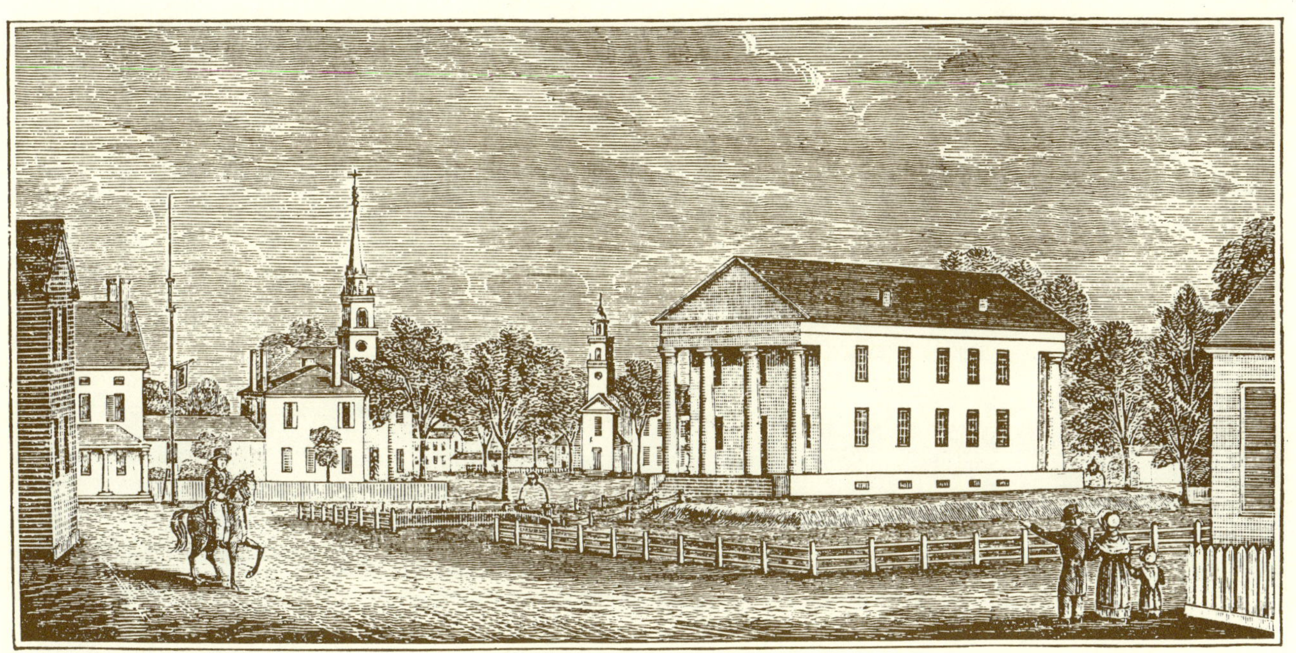

In the 19th century, Dedham could display a courthouse which served as an architectural model for public buildings. The town itself was described as desirable for both ''mechanics and men of leisure.'' The manufactories of Dedham turned out silk goods, paper, chairs, and fine straw bonnets.

Horace Mann, an early leader in the drive for strong educational systems, was born in Franklin, another fine town in Norfolk county, and the home of five cotton mills in the 1800's. Mann eventually moved to Boston, and in 1848 replaced John Q. Adams in Congress. He espoused the temperance movement, and was active in the anti-slavery cause, but his greatest dedication was to the field of education.

SNIPPET

Foxboro belonged to Stoughton until 1778. A report from the 1870's indicated that the soil was inferior, but on a more positive note, some 1,650 men and women of Foxboro turned out straw hats and bonnets worth $1,700,000 in a single year.

One of the earliest towns of the Commonwealth, Braintree was settled in 1625. It was originally called Mount Wollaston.

Wellesley College, in the town which was once called West Needham, was chartered in 1870, after affluent Henry Durant gave the college his home and his fortune. According to one historian, the pupils were to be taught not only classical languages, but also ''how to perform the duties and manage the affairs of a household.''

Katherine Lee Bates, in the 1890's, wrote of Wellesley's annual ''Float'' Day when students, faculty, friends and neighbors gathered along the shores of Lake Waban on a June night, there to enjoy boating, fireworks, and a blend of music and repartee, all of this to be a treasured memory.

The town of Milton, a mere seven miles from Boston, was taken from Dorchester in 1662. In the 1800's, paper, hats, and playing cards were made here. J.W. Barber, who drew this sketch and many others in this book, traveled on horseback across most of Massachusetts and Connecticut, plumping himself down with his easel, and sketching a quiet view of each town, while gaining some knowledge from the residents about where they lived, worked, and worshipped.

In Brookline, which was once part of Boston, the Harvard Church won notice for its use of stones from many countries. The church was built in 1873, at a cost of $100,000...Even then, Brookline had a reputation for fine scenery, roads, and gardens, and as one writer added, ''many gentlemen of taste and fortune live here.''

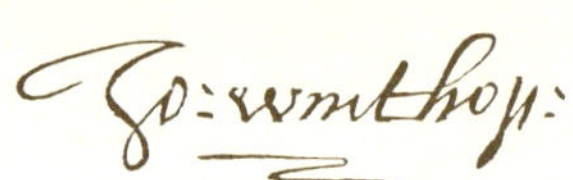

John Winthrop came from England to Salem as Governor of the Massachusetts Bay Colony in 1630, and soon established Boston as the chief community of the colony. His long tenure as governor is attributed to his ability in keeping English royalty from interfering in the colony while handling many colonial problems with tact and good judgment.

King James II appointed Edmund Andros to be Governor of New England in 1674. With the rule of Andros (shown here) came new taxes and other laws resented by the colonials.

When William of Orange landed in England in 1689, causing King James II to flee the country, Andros was made prisoner in Boston, and sent packing to England. Andros is directly in back of the drummer boy.

SNIPPET
Shawmut was the Indian name for Boston, but it was called Trimountain by the first settlers, for the three hills on which the city was built.

Seventeenth century maps such as this remain as interesting examples of early cartography, perhaps embellished by a little imagination.

In 1770, British troops of the Boston garrison killed three colonials in a street brawl. Some historians attribute this so-called Boston Massacre to some American ruffians, while the presence of the troops in itself created a rather unhappy environment. The engraving is by Paul Revere.

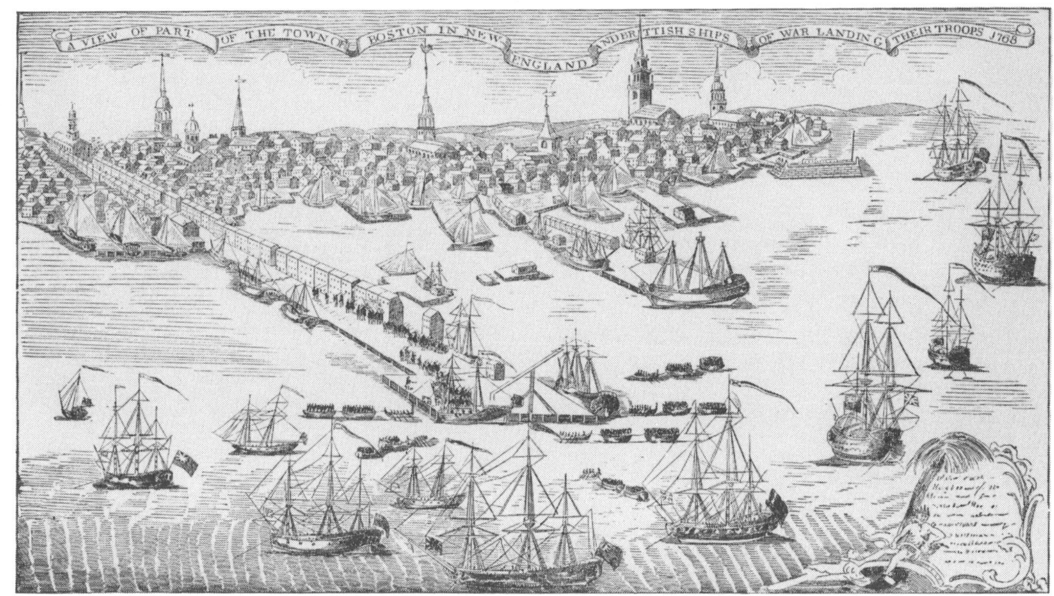

The caption for this old print of Boston Harbor reads ''British ships of war landing their troops, 1768'' — an indication that trouble was brewing.

In December of 1773, a group of colonials, disguised as Indians, boarded several English ships in Boston Harbor, tossing 342 chests of tea overboard, in protest of the new tax on tea.

An early cartoon shows England forcing America to take tea, while Justice seems appalled.

Benjamin Franklin, an outstanding diplomat, tried earnestly to build better relationships with many English leaders in London, but too often was met with indifference.

Franklin was born in 1706 in this modest home on Milk Street, Boston. It was destroyed by fire in 1811.

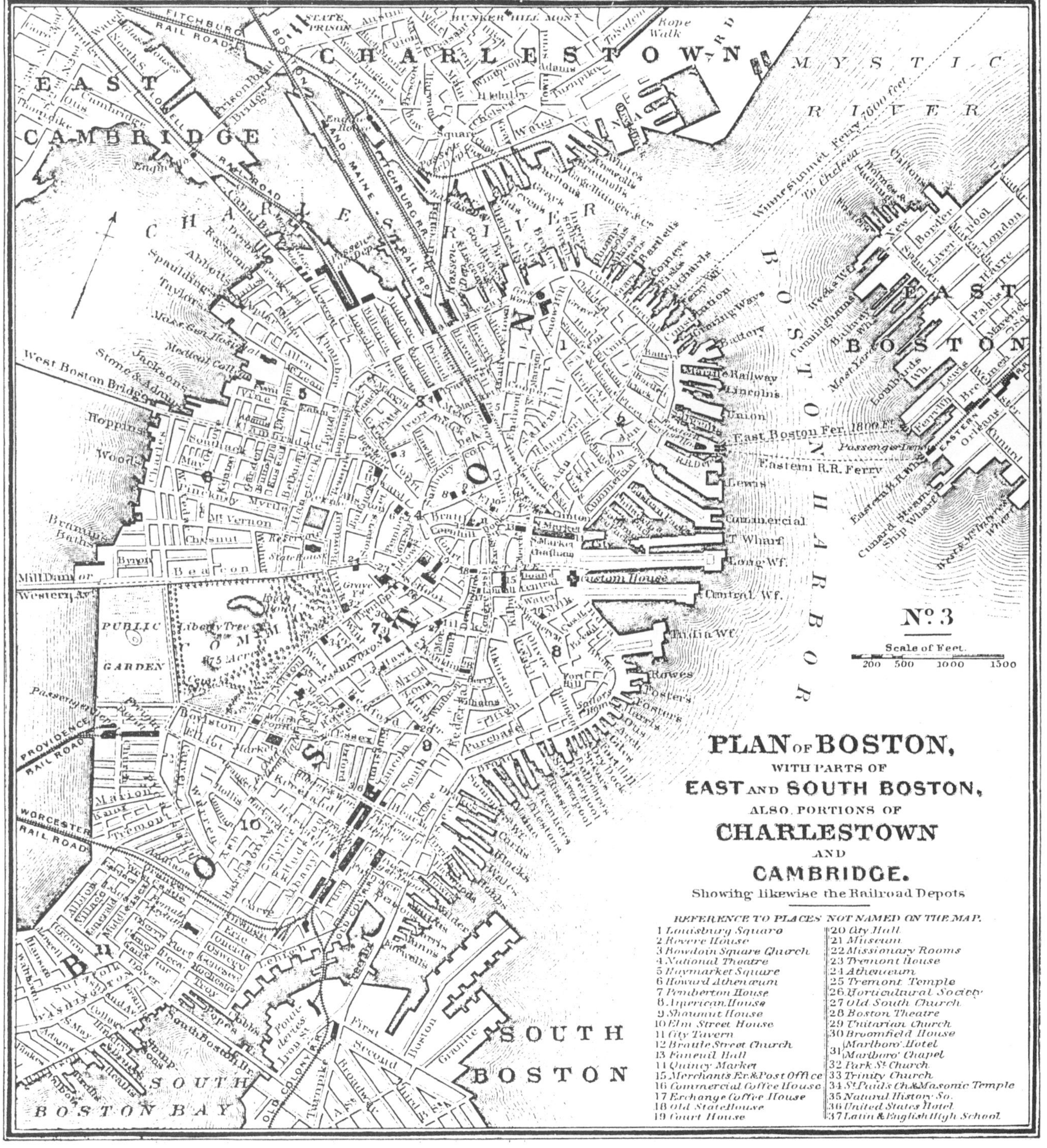

This map shows the configuration of Boston in 1848, with particular emphasis on railroad routes.

On April 11, 1775, British General Gage dispatched 800 troops to Concord via Lexington, where about seventy minute-men awaited them. When they refused to disperse, the troops under Gage opened fire, killing eight of the colonials, the actual start of hostilities.

Arriving at Concord, the British troops destroyed some military stores, but when they proceeded to the Concord Bridge, they were confronted by minute-men from Concord and Acton, forewarned by Paul Revere and others. Gunfire was exchanged, and several men from each side were killed or wounded.

Paul Revere's fame as the midnight rider who warned the villagers of the attack by troops under General Gage, was enhanced by the famous Longfellow poem which begins with ''Listen my children, and you shall hear of the midnight ride of Paul Revere.''

Paul Revere, born in 1735, was a noble horseman, but in his time was better known as a Boston copper-smith and fine engraver.

In June of 1775, the Battle of Bunker Hill, in Charlestown, marked a fierce high in the early days of the Revolution. The American forces finally retreated when their ammunition ran out, but both sides suffered heavy casualties, one historian estimating that 449 Americans and 1,055 British fell during the battle.

When George Washington took command of the American forces in July of 1775, his command post was the Craigie House in Cambridge. With some 19,000 troops under Artemus Ward at his disposal, Washington gradually gained firm control of the hills around Boston.

Bunker Hill Monument, on Breed's Hill, Charlestown, was completed in June of 1843, Daniel Webster giving an oration to mark the occasion.

40

Although John Hancock was a native of Braintree, his political success led him to this fine residence in Boston. He was elected Governor of the Commonwealth of Massachusetts for nine terms — a tribute to his patriotic efforts in the Revolution.

One of the few bright spots in our war with
Great Britain in 1812 was the victory of the
"Constitution" over the British frigate
"Guerriere." In command of "Old Ironsides"
was Captain Isaac Hull.

In his big battle with the frigate "Guerriere,"
Captain Isaac Hull of the "Constitution"
withheld fire until the last possible moment,
but then, in a fifteen minute pounding, left the
British ship a total wreck.

Horatio Alger, the novelist who won fame by
dramatizing man's heroic struggles to overcome
adversity, was born in Revere in 1834.

Nathaniel Currier, the famous lithographer, was
born in Roxbury in 1813, and the great bare-
knuckled heavyweight boxing champion, John L.
Sullivan, was also born in that town —
since 1867 a part of Boston.

Boston and many other Massachusetts cities brought forth a flood of fine writers, artists, and statesmen. Among the writers was Boston-born Edgar Allan Poe. Poe died at a young age of forty, but left us with ''Murders of the Rue Morgue'' and other lasting treasures.

Samuel G. Goodrich, another literary Bostonian, was also known as Peter Parley. He won fame for his fine children's books. Sometimes helped by his brother Charles, he completed more than two hundred books, and also gave encouragement to Nathaniel Hawthorne.

The famous poet and essayist Ralph Waldo Emerson was born in Boston, traveled abroad, and settled down in Concord. He believed that a person's individual conscience should be the judge of spiritual matters.

Edward Everett, born in Dorchester in 1794, was a notable blend of statesman, scholar, and orator. He was clergyman, professor of Greek, member of Congress, President of Harvard, Secretary of State, and the orator who preceded Lincoln at Gettysburg.

This painting, called simply "Sailboat," was the work of another 19th century Boston talent. His name was Winslow Homer, and his reputation for outstanding maritime paintings is now worldwide.

Born in 1819, Julia Ward Howe was active in the anti-slavery movement, woman's suffrage activities, and other causes. Her greatest claim to fame, however, stems from a poem she wrote in 1861, called "Battle Hymn of the Republic."

Charles Sumner, an outspoken anti-slavery statesman, was elected to the U.S. Senate in 1850 to succeed Daniel Webster. His strong views provoked a South Carolina Congressman to assault him in the Halls of Congress. Although he never recovered his physical well-being, Sumner played a major role in persuading Lincoln to issue the Emancipation Proclamation.

Congressman Brooks was fined $300 for his vicious attack on Senator Sumner but the House of Representatives could not muster the necessary two-thirds vote to expel Mr. Brooks in May of 1856. Only eight months later, Brooks was stricken from unexplained natural causes and died.

The present day State House at Beacon and Park Streets was built in 1795, at a cost of $133,000. The south side was added in 1852, and the dome gilded in 1874. Statues of Horace Mann and Daniel Webster were also added in the 19th century.

The old State House at Washington and State Streets was built in 1713. It was here that John Hancock was inaugurated as governor in 1780.

The King's Chapel, another Boston landmark, was originally an Anglican church and later Unitarian. The building was erected in 1754, and was preceded by a wooden building built in 1688. A fine organ was imported from England for the church, but a shortage of funds eliminated plans for a steeple.

Christ Church (Old North Church), shown here, is known for its tablet which says ''The signal lanterns of Paul Revere displayed in the steeple of this church April 18, 1775 warned the country of the march of the British troops to Lexington and Concord.''

The Old South Meeting House on Washington Street was built in 1729, and was the site of many colonial protest meetings in the 1770's. A building preceding this one was built in the 1670's, and was the church in which Benjamin Franklin was baptized.

$\mathbf{B}$oston's Common was established in 1634, this public park originally intended to serve as a cow pasture. The great elm shown in this early sketch gave way in 1876, but the Common remains — without the cows.

$\mathbf{P}$eter Faneuil, a prosperous merchant and patriot, had this ''Cradle of Liberty'' built in 1742, with the help of James Otis. After a fire gutted the interior in 1761, the building was rebuilt and re-opened in 1763.

$\mathbf{T}$he famous Faneuil Hall was enlarged to a width of eighty feet, and a third story added in 1806. This drawing of the great Boston landmark is by the famous artist, W.H. Bartlett.

Boston's Custom House at the foot of State Street was begun in 1837, and completed ten years later. Each granite Doric column is said to weigh forty-two tons. In 1878, the Collector of the Port, Mr. Beard, was paid $8,000 per year, while the total of wages for his 381 employees was $482,000.

In this view of the head of State Street, the old State House stands straight ahead. The "Traveller" building at the left was once the site of the "Colonial Centinel," an early newspaper. The adjoining building occupies the site where the Old First Church stood, complete with thatch roof and mud walls.

Located in Congress Square, the Exchange Coffee House was a popular place for meeting and lodging in the early 19th century. On July 4, 1817, President Monroe attended a sumptuous dinner there, along with former President Adams, and Commodores Perry and Hull. It was destroyed by one of Boston's many bad fires.

Alexander Graham Bell, a native of Edinburgh, moved to Boston in 1872, and only four years later obtained his patent for a telephone. The instruments in this old engraving are primitive, but indicate that Bell's invention limited the need for shouting over the back fence.

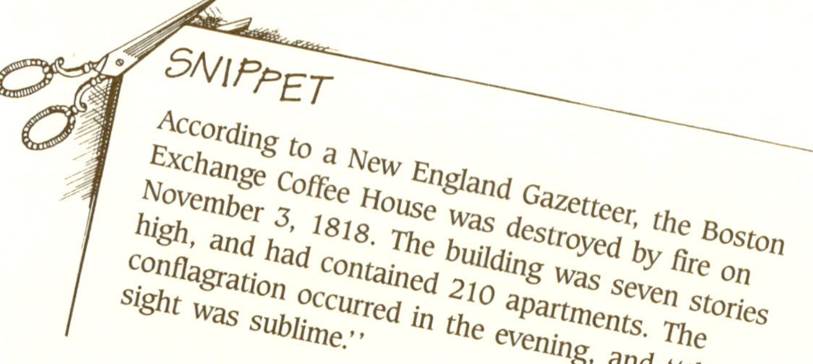

SNIPPET

According to a New England Gazetteer, the Boston Exchange Coffee House was destroyed by fire on November 3, 1818. The building was seven stories high, and had contained 210 apartments. The conflagration occurred in the evening, and "the sight was sublime."

Only a year after the great Chicago fire, Boston suffered a fate which was nearly as bad. Despite heroic efforts by firemen and citizens, the downtown Boston area suffered losses of $75,000,000, and this view portrays the awesome event of November 9, 1872.

In 1814, Jedidiah Morse noted that the chief manufactures of Boston were rum, beer, paper hangings, loaf sugar, cards, sailcloth, spermaceti, tallow candles, and glass. He also asserted that Boston had twenty distilleries.

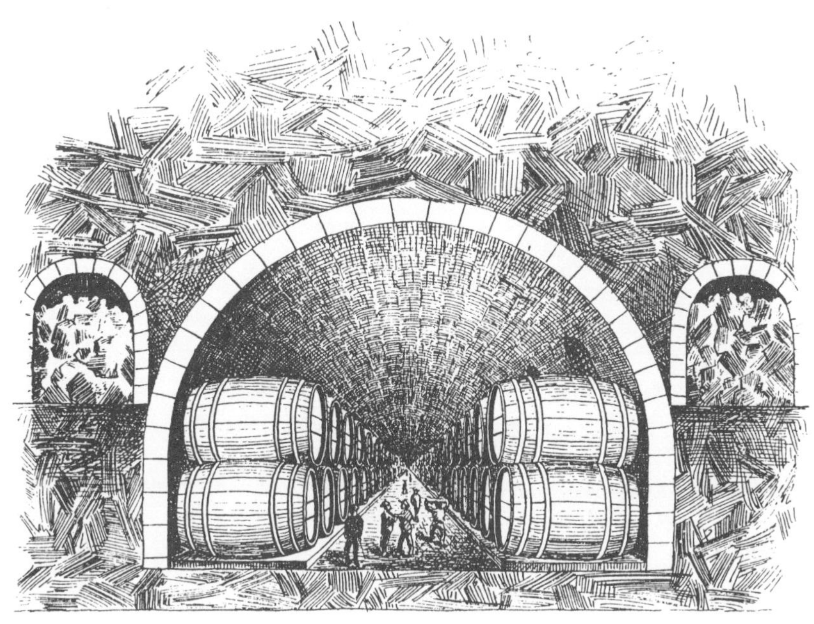

The earliest mention of a brew house in the colonies was that of one operated by Mr. Sedgewick of Boston in 1637. This is a drawing of an early storage cellar — the owner not identified.

From the pages of an 1883 "Outing" magazine we can see some of the members of Boston's first Bicycle Club — a sporting activity whose growth was phenomenal until the automobile appeared on the scene.

This handsome view of Boston Harbor appeared in an atlas of the 1880's. Sailing ships still appear to outnumber steamers, but the great years of sail were beginning to draw to a close.

The total number of vessels cleared from the port of Boston for the year ending June 30, 1855, was 1,033, with crews of 11,770. Of all ports, only New York had greater traffic.

The "Sachem" was one of many fine three-masted sailing ships built in East Boston. Launched in 1875, the ship was listed at 1312 tons — about average size for those days.

In this advertisement of 1879, the Fall River Line simply displayed one of their finest products: the luxurious sidewheeler "Bristol," whose regular voyages to New York would compete with travel by railroad.

Massachusetts Institute of Technology was incorporated in 1861, and located at that time on Boylston Street. Constructed of pressed brick, the building accommodated 300 students in 1880. Among its features was a restaurant in the gymnasium.

Ice gathering, storing, shipping and selling was a major industry in the middle of the 19th century, and this ice elevator was an important tool in the trade. By carefully covering the ice cargo with several layers of sheathing, ice could be and was sold as far distant as South America, with small melting losses. Small ponds near Boston served as sources.

The Boston University School of Medicine, on East Canal Street, opened in 1873, and admission was available to both sexes. Close by was the Massachusetts Homeopathic Hospital. Boston College, on Harrison Avenue, was founded ten years earlier, and by 1879 had 120 students.

The Parker House, according to an 1879 book, ''is famed all over America for its solid comfort and real attractions...a model of New England cleanliness.'' The wines were personally selected by Mr. Parker, and room costs ranged from $1 to $5 a day.

When this 1879 sketch of a mansion-house on Court Street appeared, the grocery store name of S.S. Pierce was prominently displayed; but other names had preceded the arrival of Mr. Pierce: In 1787, George Washington had stayed there, and at one time Daniel Webster maintained his law office in the building.

Macullar, Williams, and Parker, with a huge clothing store and factory on Washington Street in the 19th century had their piece goods made by 450 women and 100 men, ''all kept so long as they do their work faithfully — no pinched nor starved faces are seen.''

Boston merchants in the 1860's were ready to meet your every need: a cure for drunkenness, some fine hoop skirts, or special cures for rheumatism and other afflictions — all advertised in a Boston Directory.

DR. SPRING,
264 FEDERAL STREET, BOSTON,
CURES FELONS WITHOUT LANCING.

Also Abscess, Crushed Fingers, Bruises, Burns, Sore Leg,
Stiff Joints, Ulcers, Cancer, Warts, Mercurial Sores,
Fistula, Gangrene, and Mortification,

WITHOUT CUTTING OR PROBING.

INCONTESTABLE PROOF AS TO ABILITY.

DR. SPRING

Prepares, from

BARKS, ROOTS, AND HERBS,

A Medicine warranted to cleanse the Stomach and Bowels, regulate the Liver and Kidneys, and create a
healthy appetite. It is invaluable in the cure of

Scrofula, Inflammatory Rheumatism,

FEMALE IRREGULARITIES, MERCURIAL DISEASES,
Dyspepsia, Dropsy, and General Debility.

Mail Orders forwarded by Express.

GREAT DISCOVERY.
CARPEDIAM, CARPEDIAM.

Morton's Great English Remedy,

The best cure for

DRUNKENNESS

EVER DISCOVERED.

Wives save your husbands and friends; it can be
given secretly.

J. H. BOSWORTH, Sole Proprietor.
93 Hanover St., Boston, Mass.

For sale by GEO. C. GOODWIN & CO., M. S. BURR
& CO., CARTER & WILEY, and JOHN A. BURLEIGH.

GLAZIER, MAREAN, & CO.,
81 SUMMER STREET,

MANUFACTURERS OF

HOOP SKIRTS.

Importers and Jobbers of Corsets, Hoisery, Gloves,
Buttons, and Fancy Goods.

SOLE AGENTS FOR THE AMERICAN FAN COMPANY.

Manufacturers of Paper Collars and Cuffs, and Agents for the Universal Paper Collar.

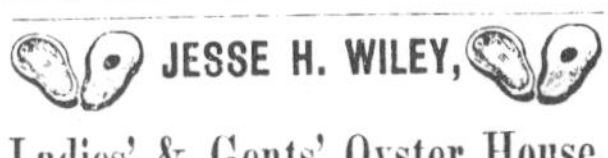

An 1867 New England Directory afforded the gourmet a wide choice of oysters, fish and groceries from several Boston sources.

Elegant hearses and airtight caskets were featured by the John Peak undertaking firm of Boston in 1868 — "just the thing for burial purposes."

Jordan, Marsh & Co.

Dry Goods.

Finest and most attractive assortment of European and American Fabrics to be found in the country.

Special bargains in forty-six distinct and separate Departments, comprising Suits, Cloaks, Shawls, Black Silks, Colored Silks, Satins & Velvets, Black Goods, Colored Dress Goods, Woolens, Small Wares, Underwear, Hosiery, Gloves, Gents' Furnishing Goods, Buttons, Umbrellas, Parasols, Worsted Goods, Hamburgs and White Goods, Fringes & Dress Trimmings, Handkerchiefs, Lace Goods, Collars & Cuffs, Ladies' Ties, Ribbons, Cottons, Linens, Flannels, Blankets & Quilts, Prints, Linings, Millinery, Ladies' Underwear, Infants' Wear, Carpets, Upholstery, Boys' Clothing, Misses' Clothing, Furs, Books, Fancy Goods, Bags, Stationery, Toilet Articles, Wrappers, Jewelry, Shoes, Embroidery Goods.

Jordan, Marsh & Co.

Washington and Avon Streets,

Boston, Mass.

Several familiar quality names appeared in the Boston Directories of the late 1800's, in such diverse areas as dry goods, restaurants, and insurance, perhaps a reminder that businesses which are with us for a hundred years or more must be doing something right.

JOHN HANCOCK
MUTUAL LIFE INSURANCE COMPANY,
41 STATE STREET, Boston.

THE whole surplus belongs to the policy-holders, and is equitably divided among them, on the contribution plan, at the end of the first year, and annually thereafter.   The distribution may be applied to the reduction of the next annual premium, or to purchase additional insurance, payable with the policy at maturity.

The third distribution, amounting to $130,000, is now being paid.

All the policy-holders of this Company are guaranteed against the forfeiture of their policies by a Statute of the State of Massachusetts.

Assets, March 1, 1868, over $1,000,000.

Amount at risk, March 1, 1868, $11,000,000,

Losses paid in the year 1867, $50,806.

GEO. B. AGER, Secretary.   GEO. P. SANGER, President.

ELIZUR WRIGHT, Actuary.

GENERAL AGENTS.

HALL & MANNING, 155 Broadway, N.Y.
DENISON, PACKER, & CO., Mystic Bridge, Conn.
HENRY E. LINCOLN, 637 Chestnut St., Phila.
HENRY R. THOMPSON, 27 Chamber of Commerce, Chicago, Ill.
PAUL & COUCH, 310 North Fifth Street, St. Louis, Mo.

One of Charlestown's finest citizens was Samuel F.B. Morse. Best known as the pioneer telegrapher, Morse was also a distinguished artist whose paintings were not widely recognized for some time. His father was Jedidiah, the geographer.

John W. Barber's view from Copp's Hill looks at Charlestown in 1839. The man's cane appears to point at Bunker Hill Monument, unfinished at that time.

In September of 1860, ''E.M.'' of Boston wrote ''Scientific American'' magazine to describe a woman from Barcelona who had circled the city on a ''bat wing'' for many miles, but was ruthlessly arrested upon landing. Neither ''E.M.'' nor the bird woman was heard from thereafter.

The United States Marine Hospital at Chelsea, just a few miles from Boston, served the needs of sick and disabled seamen during the 1800's, under the supervision of the Collector of the Port of Boston.

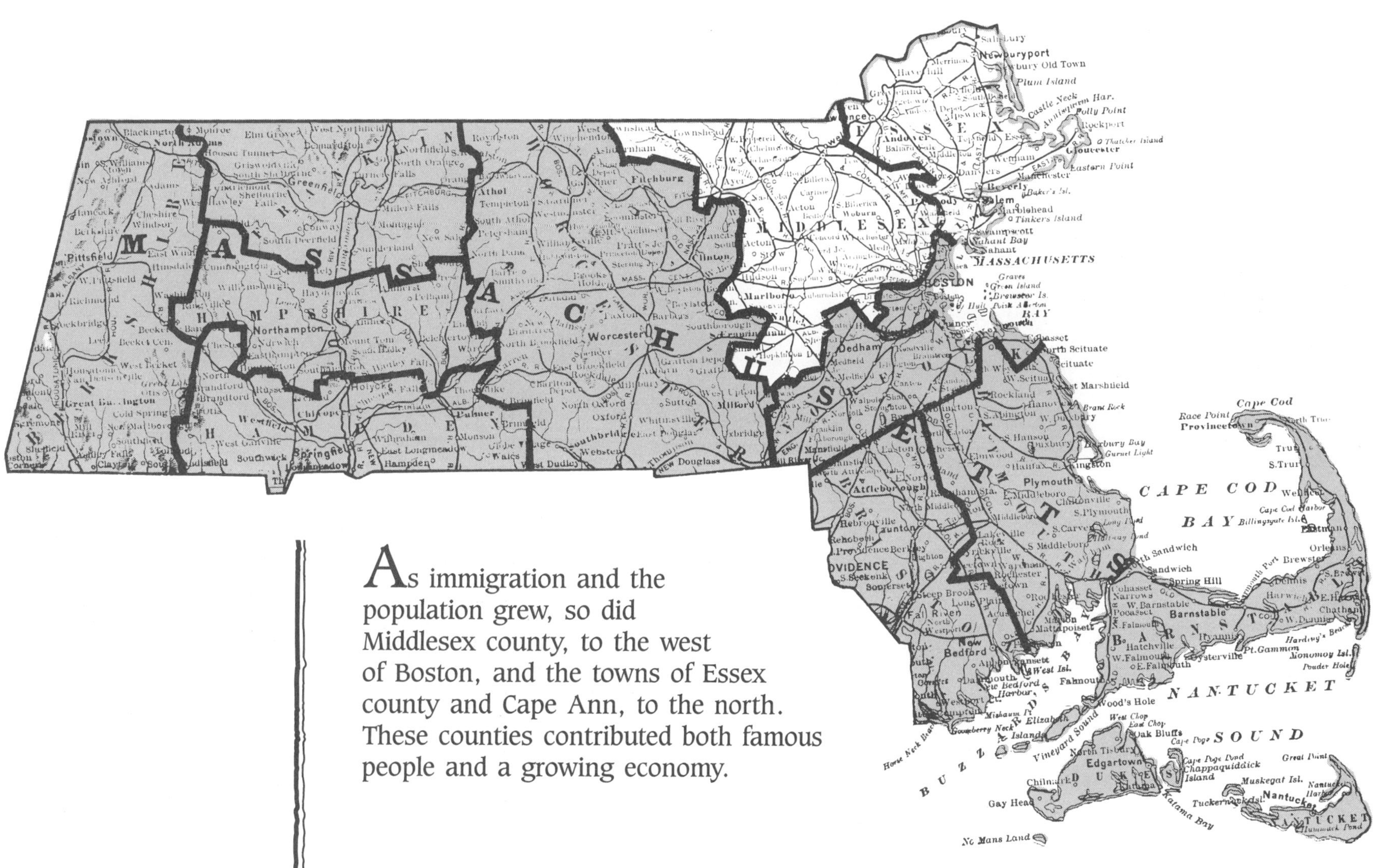

As immigration and the population grew, so did Middlesex county, to the west of Boston, and the towns of Essex county and Cape Ann, to the north. These counties contributed both famous people and a growing economy.

MIDDLESEX & ESSEX
COUNTIES

In Middlesex County, across the Charles River from Boston, lies Cambridge, the home of Harvard, whose campus shown here appeared in a school textbook of the 1800's. Cambridge is also the home of M.I.T. The whole area in and surrounding Boston has long had proper pride in both its educational and medical strengths.

Henry Wadsworth Longfellow was one of the many literary giants associated with Cambridge and Harvard. Born in Portland, Maine in 1807, he was graduated from Bowdoin with classmate Nathaniel Hawthorne, and was named Professor of Modern Language at Harvard in 1835.

The Longfellow house in Cambridge was built in 1760. Among the best-known of his writings are ''The Courtship of Miles Standish'' and ''Tales of a Wayside Inn.''

Oliver Wendell Holmes, born in Cambridge in 1809, was a much respected doctor, poet, essayist, and professor at both Dartmouth and Harvard. His son also won fame as a notable Justice of the U.S. Supreme Court.

This is the birthplace of Dr. Holmes in Cambridge. Among his writings are ''The Wonderful One Hoss Shay'' and ''The Autocrat of the Breakfast Table.''

The first settlers of Holliston arrived in 1710, and in the winter of 1753/54 the town experienced a mysterious sickness which took fifty-three lives. By 1874 Holliston was a thriving town of 3,000 inhabitants, with their factories producing nails, wrenches, pumps, and several agricultural products.

James Russell Lowell, another native of Cambridge, was born in 1819, and won recognition as a writer, critic, magazine editor, and Harvard professor. Other distinguished family members were Abbott Lawrence Lowell, President of Harvard, and Amy Lowell, a distinguished poet.

A sketch from a 19th century Harper's magazine shows the Harvard campus as it was in 1720. The Congregational minister for whom the college was named died when he was only thirty-one.

Charles Eliot had a lifelong interest in education and in science. Serving as President of Harvard from 1869 to 1909, he was a major influence in the growth of American educational standards.

A mere stone's throw from Boston, the town of Somerville was part of Charlestown until 1872, and by 1850 had a population of 8,000. The McLean Asylum for the Insane, shown here, was opened in that city in 1818, and while the name may sound unkind today, the care and rehabilitation program was thoughtful, thorough, and personalized.

SNIPPET

In the late 1860's, the Town of Tewksbury was selected as the site for an almshouse. A farm connected with this institution provided the inmates with an opportunity to do manual labor there, enhancing the town's reputation as a place where its residents could learn about a career in agriculture.

This mansion at Medford was built in 1634 for Governor Cradock of the Massachusetts Bay Company. Shipbuilding was a major industry at Medford for many years. Its people, we are advised by a writer in 1873, ''are intelligent, urbane, and progressive.''

Weston, once a part of Watertown, was considered as ''neat and flourishing'' in 1839, while a historian of 1873 added that the residents were ''temperate, intelligent, and refined.'' Homeowners in Weston paid taxes of ninety cents for every hundred dollars of assessed value.

A Gazetteer of 1839 describes Watertown as very beautiful, with neat farm houses, cottages, and delightful gardens. Mr. Barber's sketch shows the ''central part'' but not the various factories which produced boots, shoes, paper, candles, soap, and boxes.

Originally known as ''Charlestown Village,'' Woburn was incorporated in 1642. Charles B. Winn gave the town this sizable public library in the early 1800's. For many years, Woburn was a rich source of garden produce, while its factories turned out leather goods, shoes, and glue.

The rattan works at Wakefield gave employment to a thousand men and women in the 1870's. The rattan was used in the manufacture of chairs, baskets, boxes, matting, and carpeting. The town had been called Lynn Village, Reading, and South Reading, until it recognized its chief benefactor, Cyrus Wakefield, in 1868.

The Old North Bridge at Concord, where British troops had been heavily engaged by the minute-men, with substantial losses by both sides, back in 1775.

The Massachusetts House was built in 1876 for the great Centennial Exhibition at Philadelphia, serving as an elegant display of architecture for commissioners and visitors. It was subsequently moved to Lexington.

Henry David Thoreau, the author and naturalist, was born at Concord, and built his cabin at nearby Walden Pond, where he lived alone for two years.

Daniel Chester French, the great sculptor, born in 1850, moved to Concord when he was seventeen, later creating the "Minute Man" in that town, and other fine monuments in many cities.

Nathaniel Hawthorne, author of "The House of Seven Gables" and many other fine works, lived in Concord's "Old Manse" for several years. He spent a greater part of his life in Salem.

The central part of Concord was sketched by J.W. Barber in the peaceful days of 1839. At the right are the Unitarian church and the Middlesex Hotel.

Bronson Alcott was a close friend of Ralph Waldo Emerson, and a brilliant philosopher and educator who, despite these strengths, was frequently poor until he founded his Concord School of Philosophy, and shared his daughter's success.

Louisa May Alcott, the daughter of Bronson Alcott, and a good friend of Emerson and Thoreau, achieved notice for her Civil War writings, became editor of the Merry's Museum magazine, and won true fame as the author of ''Little Women.''

Jedidiah Morse, in 1804, wrote that Sudbury had some 856 inhabitants, while a Gazetteer of 1873 took particular note of Longfellow's Old Wayside Inn, shown here, which was licensed in 1666. Its popularity and reputation have continued to the present day, well beyond the 300 years since its licensing.

In 1839, artist Barber took note of Waltham's Massasoit Hotel, as sketched here. In 1884, another historian had praise for the Prospect House of the same town. Waltham by that time had a population of 8,000 and a well-known watch factory with 800 employees.

In the 1830's, Bedford had a population of 858, some of whose residents produced 90,000 pairs of shoes per year.

The growing town of Framingham in the 1870's, claimed not only this fine state normal school, but a good public house (hotel), weekly journal, a farmer's club, two high schools, a post of the G.A.R., a Masonic Lodge, eight churches, and a population of 8,000. It was described as ''one of the most beautiful towns of the Commonwealth.''

The Laselle Seminary, as pictured here, was founded at Newton in 1825, to foster the training of Baptist ministers. The town grew slowly in its early years, but by 1873 counted 16,000 residents.

Incorporated in 1781, Natick was the birthplace of Henry Wilson, vice-president of the United States under Ulysses S. Grant. Calvin Stowe, sometimes referred to as the husband of Harriet Beecher Stowe, was also a native of Natick.

SNIPPETS

In 1804, the town of Wilmington had 797 residents, many of them raising hops. By 1839, the population suffered a net loss of two, but the hop crops from 1806 to 1837 weighed more than sixteen million pounds, for which growers received an average price of thirteen cents per pound.

In 1874, Winchester had 2,645 residents, excellent public schools, and ''an air of comfort, thrift, and independence.''

Malden, shown here in 1839, had grown to 7,400 people by 1873. Its manufactories produced dress trimmings, metal pipes, patent leather, palm leaf hats, and perfumery. That year the town appropriated $26,000 for the support of its public schools.

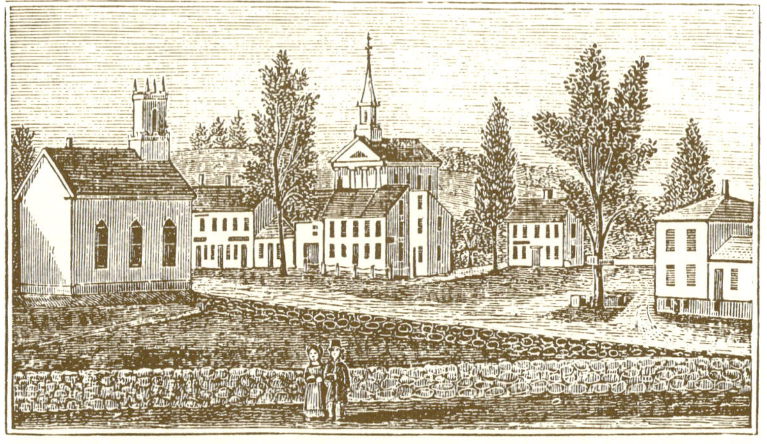

An 1804 Gazetteer describes Marlborough as ''ancient and wealthy.'' Incorporated in 1660, it developed into a substantial farming town, providing ''fat cattle, pork, fruit, and all varieties of the dairy.'' By the 1870's, Marlborough could claim seven churches, including the two shown here.

SNIPPETS

Billerica was settled in 1653, and suffered severe losses during the era of the French and Indian Wars. By the middle of the 19th century, the town was busy turning out bed binding, soft soap, knives, and spirits.

The town of Burlington had 522 residents in 1837, and thirty-six years later had gained only a hundred more people. Many of them grew rye and hops. Substantial growth would have to wait for many years.

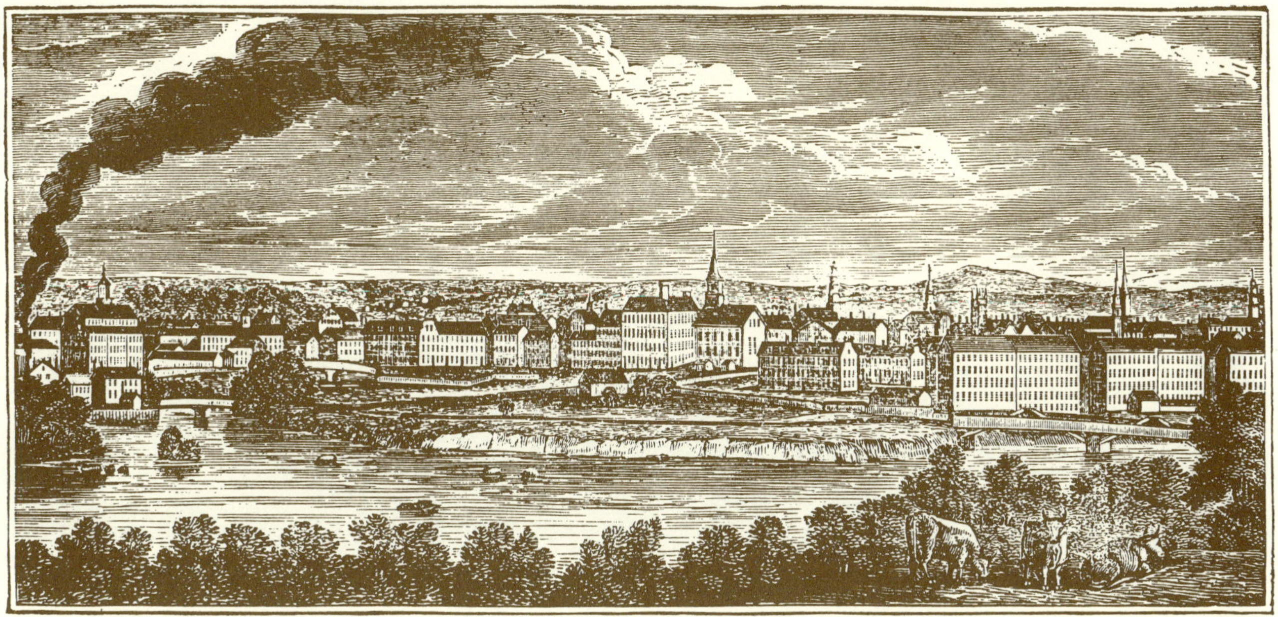

One of the largest cities of Massachusetts, Lowell, back in 1815 was a mere handful of people, but soon thereafter began its rapid growth. When J.W. Barber made this sketch in 1839, Lowell was a thriving city of 18,000 people.

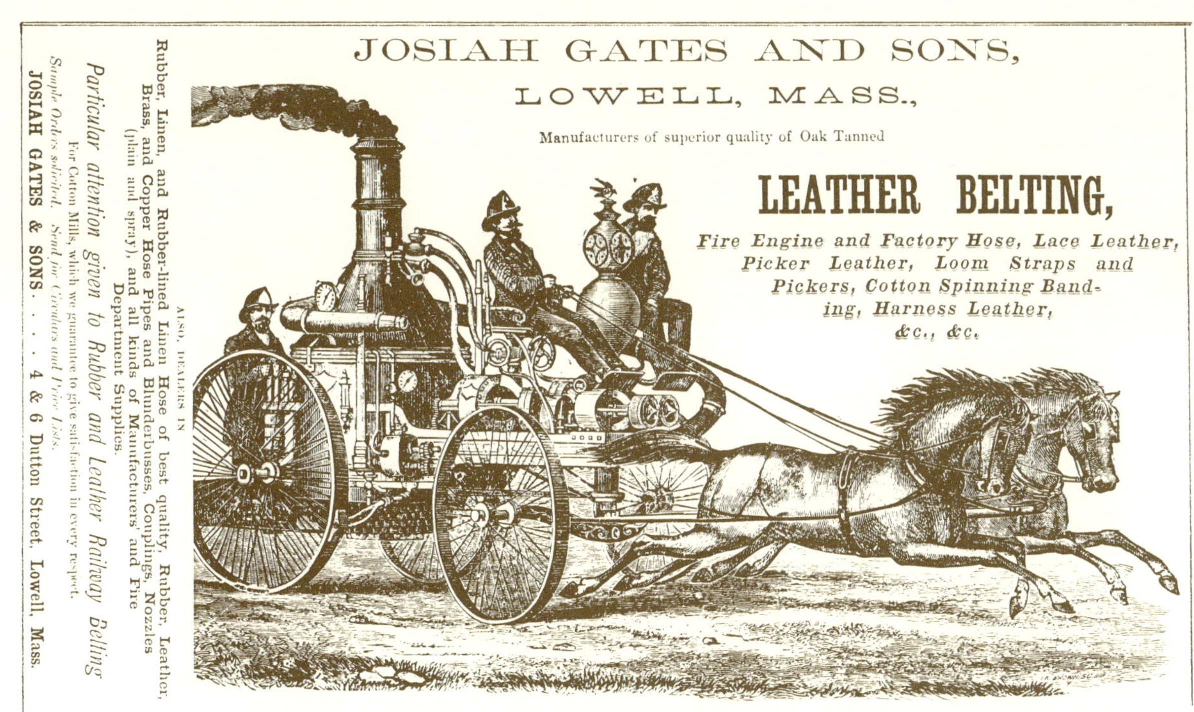

The making of leather belting and fire hoses, as advertised by the Gates Company in a New England Directory of 1875, was only one of the diversified industries which prompted people to refer to Lowell as the ''Manchester of America.''

In describing the large granite county jail of Lowell in the late 19th Century, one historian observed that it was "the finest looking building in the place." No poll was taken of the jail residents.

Another considerable asset in Lowell's rapid growth was this "very handsome courthouse," which cost $100,000 in the 1800's.

SNIPPET

Just a few miles from Lowell, Chelmsford was settled in 1653, along the south side of the Merrimack River. The people of Chelmsford, we are told by a writer of 1874, are "industrious, intelligent, and temperate."

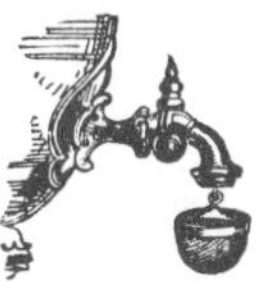

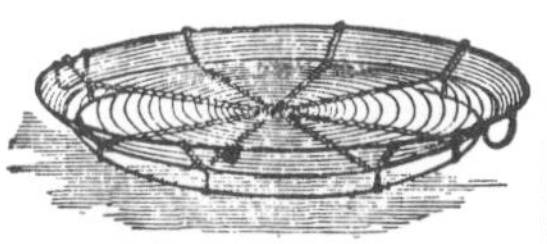

One of Lowell's famous sons was James A.M. Whistler. Some critics cited his ''peculiar theories of art,'' but his skills at etching were virtually beyond question. The painting is the famous one of Whistler's mother.

A Directory of 1867 offers the buyer considerable choice in the wide array of Lowell products, including assorted strainers, inks, dyes, and hardware. Few cities could match Lowell in the growth of its manufacturing output.

The settlement of Lynn, sketched in this 19th century view, began in 1629, shortly after the settlement of Salem, and slightly before Boston.

J. W. Barber is credited with this 1839 sketch of Lynn, one of the largest cities of Essex county. Court records of 1637 reveal one simple change from the town's former name: "Saugust is called Lin."

Mary Baker Eddy managed to buy this modest home at 12 Broad Street in Lynn, renting all of it but the parlor and an upstairs attic bedroom, where she studied and wrote, before she founded the Church of Christ, Scientist.

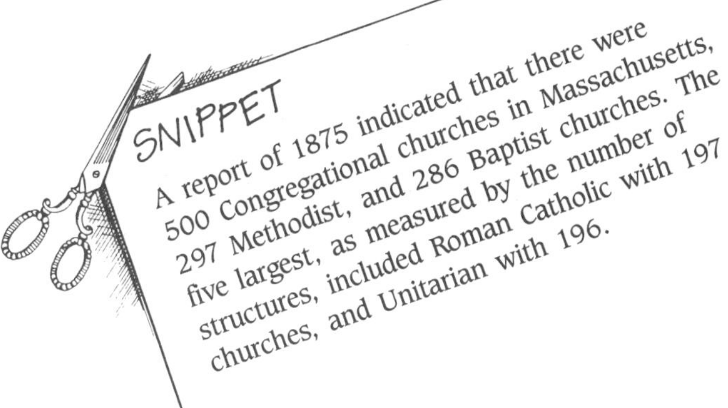

The First Congregational Church of Lynn was built in 1682, and remodeled in 1827. It was called ''The Old Tunnel...'' The sinners in the stocks remain anonymous.

Sawyer's shirts, and sewing machines by Singer and Howe appear in this 1867 advertisement. The textile industry of Massachusetts prospered in part because of the increased mechanization not found in Europe at that time.

An old government publication recounts the leading role of the 19th century Lynn shoe industry, showing us these ''modern boots and shoes.'' In the single year of 1877, Lynn factory workers turned out more than fourteen million pairs of shoes.

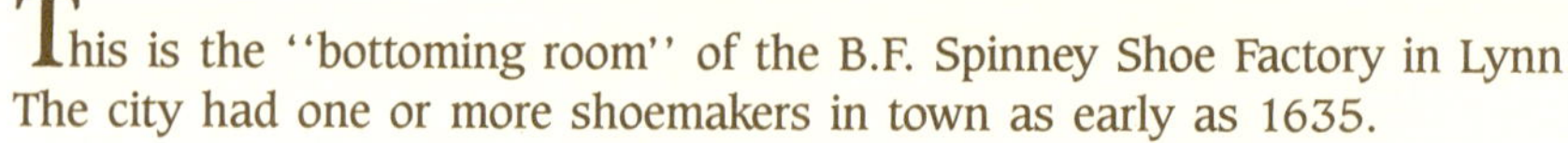

This is the ''bottoming room'' of the B.F. Spinney Shoe Factory in Lynn. The city had one or more shoemakers in town as early as 1635.

Lynn's coastal location made this a popular recreation area, as evidenced by this 19th century sketch of the Lynn Yacht Club. Earlier, a single year brought a catch of mackerel, cod, and halibut of 4,600,000 pounds for Lynn fisheries.

The small town of Nahant, long considered as a delightful health and recreation resort, offered this ''spacious and elegant'' hotel as early as 1839. Two steamboats provided daily service to and from Boston.

Swampscott, just north of Lynn, gradually changed from a hamlet for fishermen to a popular resort for sea breezes and sea bathing, as the later 1800's arrived. In the background is the ''Ocean House,'' a popular place in the 1860's.

Henry Wadsworth Longfellow discovered the beauty of seaside Nahant. This drawing shows his summer residence as it appeared in Leslie's Monthly in 1860.

This is Gregory Street, Marblehead, about 1874. The attractive town was incorporated in 1649, when only forty-four families resided there. It remains as one of the most picturesque towns of Essex county.

One of Marblehead's most prestigious sons was Elbridge Gerry, a signer of the Declaration of Independence, Governor of Massachusetts, and Vice-President under Madison.

Marblehead for many years was a leading fishing port. This drawing shows the drying of fish at Little Harbor. In 1837, more than five hundred men worked for the cod and mackerel fisheries.

The Old North Congregational Church at Marblehead. This drawing appeared in an 1874 issue of Harper's Monthly magazine.

This is Tucker's Wharf, along the rocky coast at Marblehead. One 19th century author described the area as ''an excellent place to watch a raging ocean storm.''

The pillory was one of several devices used in the 17th century to heap scorn and punishment on those who indulged in breaking the rules for proper Sabbath behavior.

Salem, shown in this rooftop sketch, was settled in 1628 by Governor Endicott, and is second to Plymouth in its antiquity. Jedidiah Morse, the great geographer, tells us that Salem had 12,613 inhabitants in 1810.

The central part of Salem appears in this sketch by J.W. Barber. Washington and Court streets are in view, while the courthouse stands in front of the carriage.

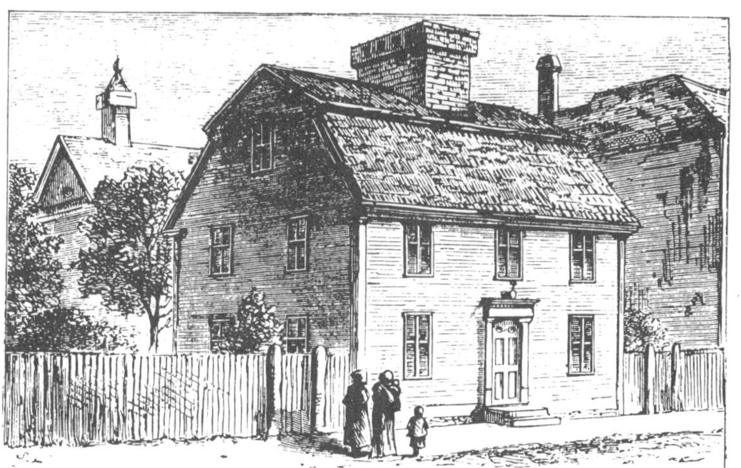

Cotton Mather was born in Boston, and was serving as a minister when he was only twenty. Sadly, he encouraged the witchcraft persecutions which culminated with the hangings in the Salem area in 1692. Rational thought prevailed, but only after torture and nineteen hangings and one pressing.

In 1692, John Proctor, leading Salem area citizen and man of great probity, denounced the witchcraft mania as utterly cruel and wicked. His wife escaped by the skin of her teeth, but Mr. Proctor paid for his temerity with his life.

The Salem Custom House, at the head of Derby Wharf, ''has always been a busy place,'' according to a historian writing in 1839, who added that Salem ''has a good harbor, good anchorage…in point of wealth and commerce it has always ranked as the second town of New England.''

Nathaniel Hawthorne was born in this home on Union Street, Salem in 1804. (See also Concord).

Danvers was originally a part of Salem. Its most famous native was Israel Putnam, who played an important part in several battles of the Revolution, and before that, in the defense from French and Indian attacks.

This state normal school, and such ongoing institutions as the Essex Institute and Peabody Museum, are refreshing reminders of the many longtime assets of Salem, where cultural, educational, and historical values have outweighed the ancient identification of witches with this fine city.

SNIPPET

Peabody, once a part of Salem, and later belonging to South Danvers, came into its own as a town in 1855, with a population of 7,343. Peabody's chief industries included the tanning and currying of hides, and the manufacture of gum, glue, and woolen goods.

Beverly, just north of Salem, was incorporated in 1668. By the year 1836, this community was producing 12,000 bushels of Indian corn, 14,000 bushels of grain, and more vegetables than the town could consume. The bridge from the south leads to Salem.

As early as 1624, an English company established a fishing station at Gloucester, and although this small group moved to Salem, Gloucester was soon earning its reputation as a leading fishing port.

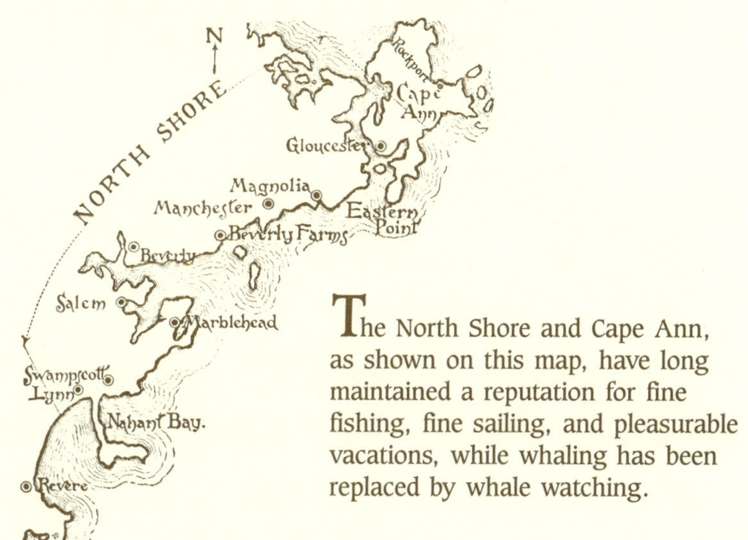

The North Shore and Cape Ann, as shown on this map, have long maintained a reputation for fine fishing, fine sailing, and pleasurable vacations, while whaling has been replaced by whale watching.

Manchester, a few miles south of Gloucester, was once a flourishing fishing town, but by the 1830's fishing had given ground to factories making chairs and cabinets.

This Gloucester Meeting House was built in 1713, and demolished in 1848. The first church in the town was started in 1642.

In this 1886 drawing from Century magazine, fishing schooners still dominate the Gloucester scene, with cod and mackerel providing a livelihood for many families.

The life of a fisherman called for hearty food, moments of peril, the uncertain rewards of the catch, and a rugged style of living which requires both respect for and love of the sea — all of this personified by the sailors of Gloucester.

One of the many pretty towns on Cape Ann is Pigeon Cove, whose harbor is shown in this sketch. The perils of fishing were all too obvious off the Gloucester and Cape Ann waters. In 1873, 28 vessels were lost in just nine months, with the loss of 172 lives, leaving 200 widows and orphans in the Gloucester area.

In 1875, Harper's pictured the Lobster Cove at Annisquam, on Cape Ann. The charm has remained for all of these years.

In 1839, J.W. Barber made this drawing of Ipswich, which is some ten miles south of Newburyport. In 1814 Jedidiah Morse noted that the town's four parishes had a population of 3,569; and back in 1614 Captain John Smith wrote that ''there are okes, pines, walnuts, and other wood to make this place an excellent habitation.''

This 1839 view of Newburyport from the north bank of the Merrimack River reveals an old suspension bridge, at the right. New Hampshire is only a few miles away, and in the early colonial days the coastal areas as far north as Portsmouth were part of Massachusetts as was the "District of Maine."

A great shipbuilding center for many years, Newburyport remains a proud and attractive city. A hundred years ago, one writer wrote that the citizens are noted for high-toned morality, intelligence, and urbanity.

Jacob Perkins, born in Newburyport in 1766, using his considerable mechanical talents, built a business which used a new method of plating shoe buckles, then invented a new single-process nail-making machine. His bathometer measured water depth, his pleometer the rate at which ships travel through water. His inventiveness was later welcomed in both France and England.

JOHN PEARSON, JR.,

WHOLESALE AND RETAIL

BAKER.

ALL KINDS OF BREAD, CAKE AND PASTRY

Constantly on hand and to order.

ESSEX WHARF,

NEWBURYPORT, ... MASS.

AMERICAN UNION

BITTERS,

A sure cure for Jaundice, Dyspepsia, Worms, Weakness, Flatulency, Bilious Diseases, and Diseases arising from an impure state of the blood. In cases of General Debility it has no superior.

Being composed entirely of Roots and Herbs, which are so compounded as to act entirely on the system, it purifies the blood, and imparts an energy and tone to the digestive organs without injury to the patient. Free from all injurious ingredients, it may be given to children, or persons of the most delicate habits. Every class of Invalids will find this an invaluable Medicine.

GEORGE W. FELCH & CO., Proprietors,
NEWBURYPORT, MASS.

Also, sole proprietors of

DR. EMMONS' CELEBRATED RHEUMATIC LINIMENT.

All Orders sent by Mail promptly attended to.

OFFICE, 31 STATE STREET, P. O. BOX 464.

Also, agents for

DR. BICKNELL'S SYRUP.

Dr. Bicknell's Syrup cures Dysentery, Diarrhœa, Cholera, Cholera Morbus, Pain or Cramp in the Stomach. E. SUTTON, Proprietor, PROVIDENCE, R. I.

C. A. NOLCINI,	DANIEL B. WHITING'S
SHIP & FAMILY DRUGGIST,	**HAIRDRESSING SALOON,**
No. 4 State Street,	NO. 31 STATE STREET,
NEWBURYPORT, MASS.	NEWBURYPORT, MASS.
Having superior facilities for the business, is prepared to	HAIR CUTTING, SHAVING,
GRIND OR PULVERIZE,	SHAMPOOING, CURLING.
As may be required,	Particular attention paid to
DRUGS, MEDICINAL HERBS, &c.,	
In the most thorough and careful manner.	
PATRONAGE SOLICITED.	CUTTING LADIES' & CHILDREN'S HAIR.

In Newburyport, if one overindulged in Pearson's pastries, he or she could seek relief from American Union bitters, visit druggist Nolcini, or have a shampoo at Whiting's Hair Saloon.

William Lloyd Garrison, born in Newburyport in 1805, was a leading abolitionist, denouncing slavery long before the public shared his views. Like Henry Ward Beecher, Garrison spent some time in England on anti-slavery campaigns.

This is the William Lloyd Garrison home in Newburyport. Although he was frequently subject to physical threats, and was once jailed for libel, Garrison continued to speak out, and lived to see the emancipation of the slaves. The state of Massachusetts was among the first to outlaw slavery.

Amesbury, on the north shore of the
Merrimack River, between Newburyport and
Haverhill, was the home of the Quaker poet,
John Greenleaf Whittier. The home, declared one
writer, ''has an air of neatness, simplicity,
and peace.''

Poet J.G. Whittier was born in Haverhill in
1807. He joined William Lloyd Garrison in
fighting slavery, and in his poetic writings, was
an admirer of Robert Burns. He won considerable
notice through such works as ''Snowbound'' and
''The Barefoot Boy.''

Haverhill, according to Jedidiah Morse, writing in
1804, ''has three distilleries, one of which has
recently undergone a laudable transmutation into a
brewery.'' Sailcloth manufacture was started in
Haverhill in 1789. In 1804 the town had a
population of 2,730, and four churches, three of
which were Congregational.

Abbott Lawrence (shown here) and his brother Amos were very successful Boston textile merchants, and the men for whom the city of Lawrence was named. Abbott Lawrence was also a philanthropist, a member of Congress, and minister to Great Britain 1849-1852.

Robert Frost, the distinguished American poet, lived in Lawrence, and worked at a textile mill before winning notice for his fine poetic New England scenes.

Textile plants like the Washington Mills, whose dress goods are promoted in this 1867 advertisement, were at the heart of the rapid growth of the city of Lawrence. Incorporated in 1847, the city made good use of the water power available through the construction of a huge dam on the Merrimack River.

E. R. MUDGE, SAWYER & CO.,

SELLING AGENTS.

BOSTON.	NEW YORK.	PHILADELPHIA.
15 Chauncy St.	43 & 45 White St.	230 Chestnut St.

Washington Mills, Lawrence, Mass.

DRESS GOODS.

PLAIN COLORS.	MIXTURES.
22 in. ALPACA.	22 in. SPRING MIXTURES.
22 in. CORDED ALPACA.	22 in. CRETONNE MIXTURES.
22 in. CRETONNE.	26 in. CRETONNE MIXTURES.
26 in. ALPACA.	**PLAIDS.**
26 in. CRETONNE.	26 in. SAINT MARIE PLAIDS.
26 in. SUPER CRETONNE. No. 500.	26 in. PARIS POPLIN.

The Washington Mills was awarded a **SILVER MEDAL** by the FRANKLIN INSTI-TUTE, Philadelphia, in October, 1874, for superiority in color of their dress good fabrics, and a silver medal had previously been given by the **Massachusetts Charitable Mechanic Association** for the excellence of their Worsted Dress Goods, Poplin Plaids, and Shawls.

The manufacture of paper was another basic industry for Lawrence in the 1850's. In this drawing we see the calender room of the Lawrence Paper Company, about 1855. The land for the city was taken from the neighboring towns of Methuen and Andover.

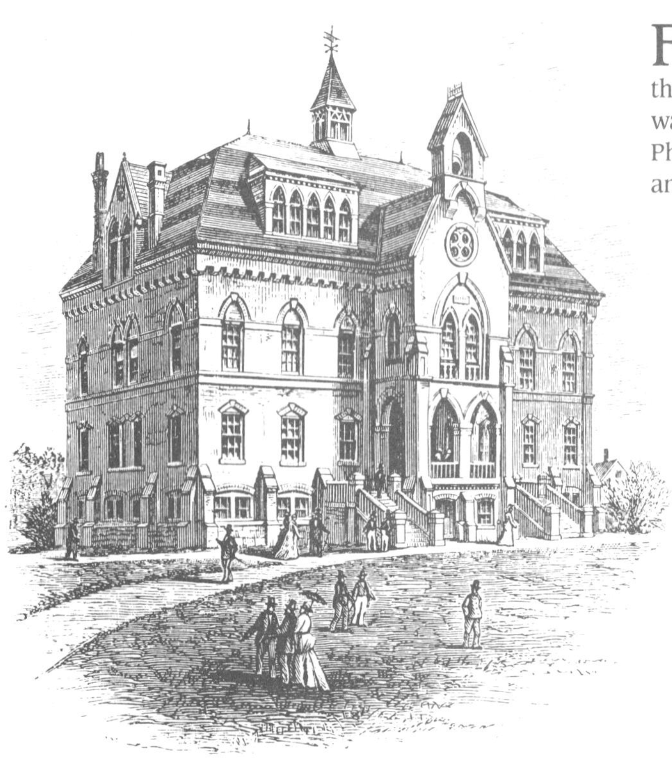

Further enhancing the educational strengths of the town, the Andover Theological Seminary was established in 1807. Both this school and Phillips maintained strong libraries, faculties, and noteworthy reputations.

Phillips Academy at Andover was incorporated in 1780, thanks to the efforts of Samuel and John Phillips and their father. The building pictured here was built in 1819, and the declared object of the school was to promote piety and virtue.

This "new" building at Phillips Academy was featured in Harper's monthly in 1877. The Abbot Female Academy was established nearby, in 1829, and was combined with Phillips late in the 20th Century.

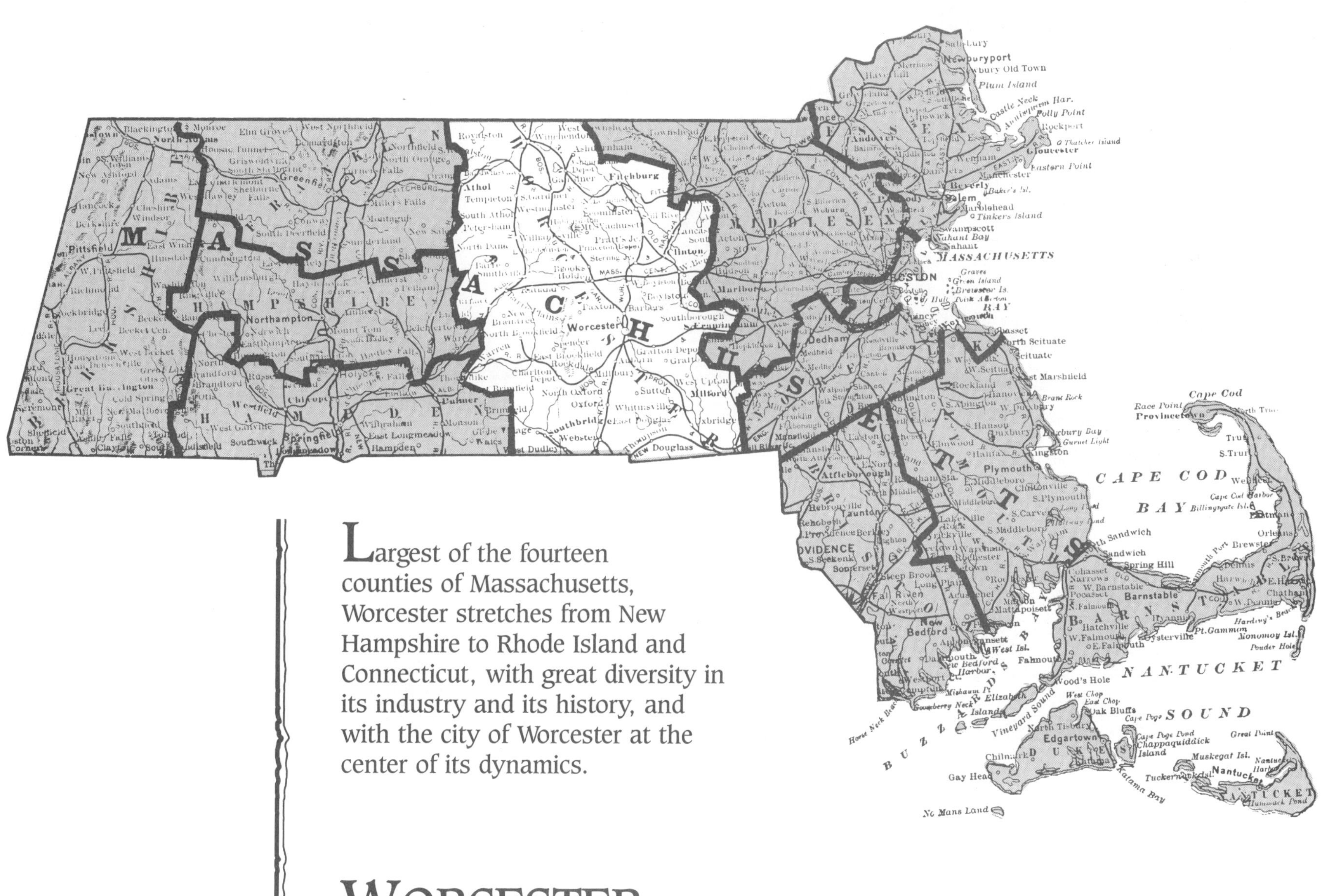

Largest of the fourteen counties of Massachusetts, Worcester stretches from New Hampshire to Rhode Island and Connecticut, with great diversity in its industry and its history, and with the city of Worcester at the center of its dynamics.

WORCESTER
C O U N T Y

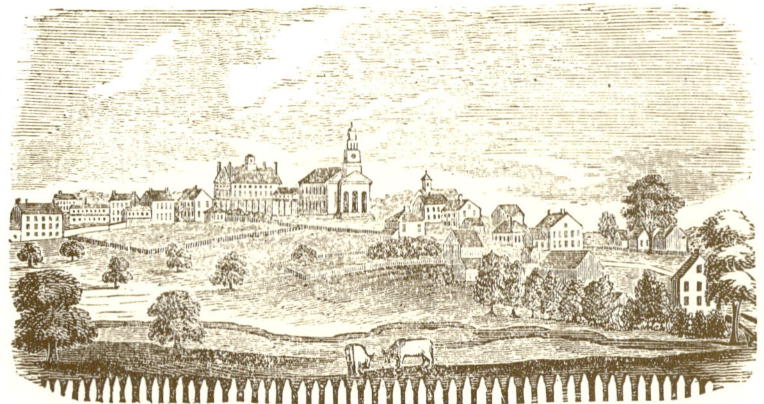

Lancaster, some fifteen miles north of Worcester, was settled in 1643, and suffered from Indian raids in 1676. By 1837, Lancaster was supported by cotton mills and the manufacture of palm-leaf hats and pianos.

Westborough, a few miles east of Lancaster, is the town where Eli Whitney was born in 1765. His invention of the cotton gin revolutionized the textile industry — especially in Massachusetts.

This is the birthplace of Eli Whitney in Westborough. His design and manufacture of interchangeable parts for machinery speeded the nation's industrial success. In later years, Whitney manufactured firearms in Connecticut.

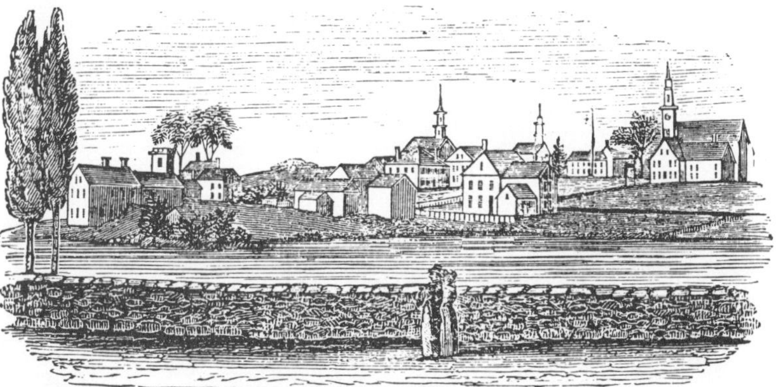

This is Mr. Barber's sketch of Milford in 1839, when the town's population was 1,637. By 1873, Milford had grown to 10,000 residents, and could boast many successful farms, and large boot and shoe factories — some manufacturers being cited for "neatness, order, and style of workmanship."

Late in the 19th century, the American Bedstead Company promoted its "dainty beds" made in Westborough. And in 1873, a historian noted that Westborough's "State Reform School for both sexes is beautifully situated on Chauncey Road."

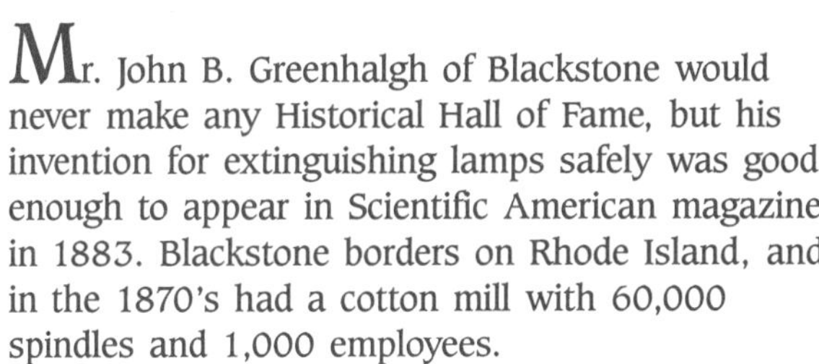

Mr. John B. Greenhalgh of Blackstone would never make any Historical Hall of Fame, but his invention for extinguishing lamps safely was good enough to appear in Scientific American magazine in 1883. Blackstone borders on Rhode Island, and in the 1870's had a cotton mill with 60,000 spindles and 1,000 employees.

Main Street, Worcester, in 1839. Settled
in 1684, long after Lancaster, Brookfield,
Springfield and Northampton, Worcester for
many years has been second only to Boston in
the size of its population. In this view, the old
South Church is at the right.

St. Paul's Roman Catholic Church was described
as ''the most magnificent church in Worcester''
by a Gazetteer of 1873. It was built of granite.
The city was often called ''The Heart of
the Commonwealth.''

The Oread Institute at Worcester resembles a feudal castle, but was used in the 1800's as a ladies seminary.

Worcester's Institute of Industrial Science, a "free school of technology," was founded through the generosity of John Boynton and other philanthropists, aided by a $50,000 grant from the Commonwealth.

Isaiah Thomas of Worcester was the pioneer printer of New England, publishing the first newspaper in that city. His press was set up three days before the Battle of Lexington, in 1775.

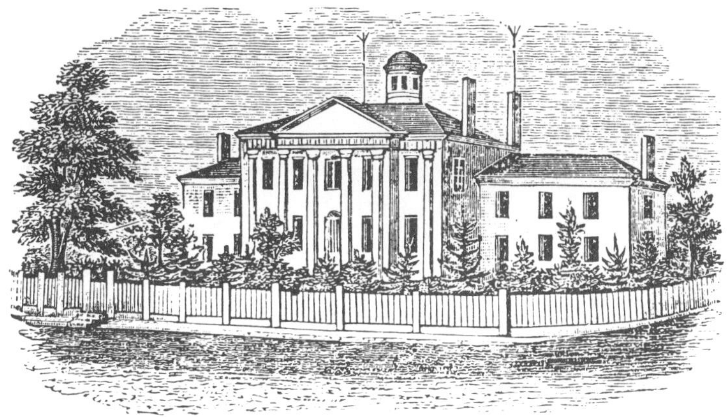

Thanks in particular to the interest and generosity of Isaiah Thomas, the Antiquarian Hall was built in 1820, marking the creation of a great storehouse of books and manuscripts of lasting national value.

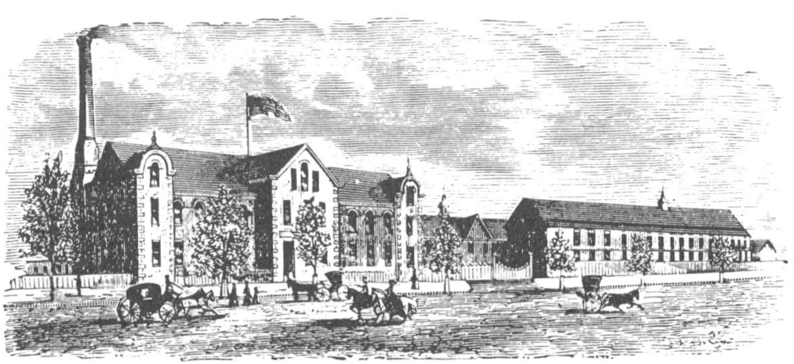

The Crompton Loom Works at Worcester, from an old print. By 1837, Worcester had eight wool and three cotton mills, four hat factories, two paper mills, and a population of 7,117.

The State Lunatic Hospital at Worcester was built in 1831 — a monument to the charitable character of the people of Massachusetts. John Hayward, writing in 1839, called it a ''model for similar institutions in other states,'' with a 56% recovery rate.

Barrows Mussey, a fine 20th century New England author, reported that this rainy regatta between the crews of Yale and Harvard, took place many years ago in Worcester — presumably on neutral ground.

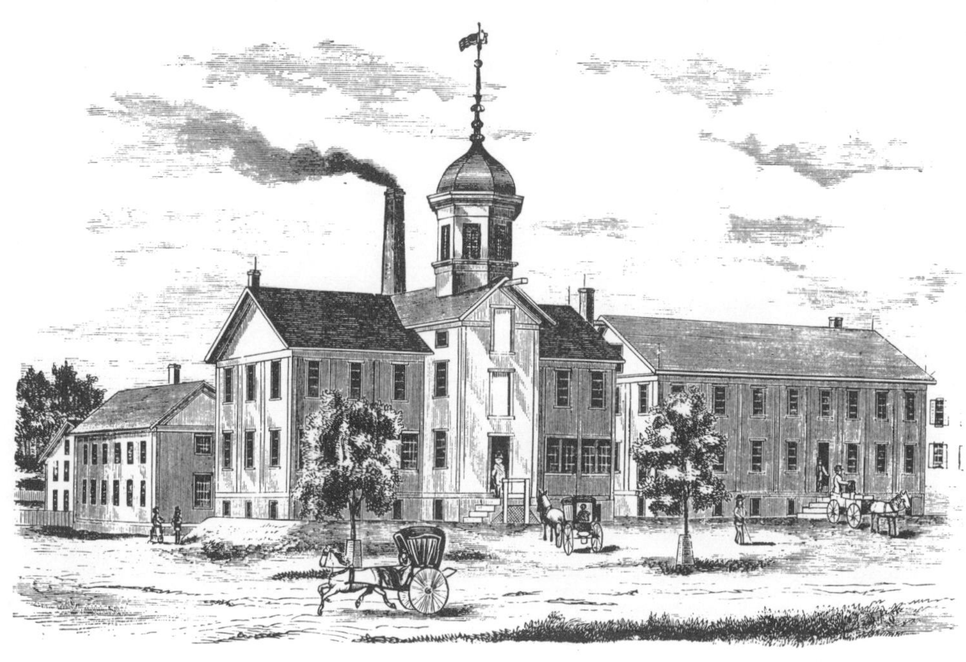

This is the screw wrench factory of the A.G. Coes Company at Worcester. A combination of good railroad lines and adequate water power speeded the growth of the city.

JOHN WILLIAMS,

MANUFACTURER OF ALL KINDS OF

GEAR WHEELS,

PATTERNS FOR CAST GEARS,

MADE OF WOOD OR IRON.

Particular attention given to

CUTTING FINISHED WORK.

Also, Drawings for Gear Work made to order.

No. 3 CYPRESS ST., WORCESTER, MASS.

The diversity of Worcester is reflected by these advertisements offering everything from gear wheels to teas, spice, and coffee. Among the assets of the area, according to one historian, were "industrious and intelligent people, a salubrious climate, and fertile soil."

BAY STATE COFFEE AND SPICE MILLS.

STOCKWELL & JOSLIN,

DEALERS IN

Teas, Coffees, Spices,

CREAM TARTAR, MUSTARD, SOAPS, &C.

Office and Salesroom, 10 Foster Street,

MILLS, CORNER EXCHANGE AND UNION,

WORCESTER, MASS.

Six miles east of Worcester is Shrewsbury,
joined with the former city by a bridge 525 feet
long, costing all of $6,000...Shrewsbury
products included straw bonnets, guns, hats,
chairs, and boots and shoes.

Oxford, ten miles south of Worcester, was
settled by a group of French Protestants in 1686.
This sketch by Barber in 1839 shows the
remnants of a fort on nearby Mayo's Hill, built
after an Indian raid of 1696 all but wiped out
the settlement.

Clara Barton

Clara Barton was born in Oxford in 1821. She
was a dedicated teacher for ten years, and won
greater notice through her devotion to the
care of wounded soldiers in the Civil War. It was
she who founded the American Red Cross, and
her entire career was devoted to those needing
help in one way or another.

SNIPPET
Named after DeWitt Clinton, the town of
Clinton was taken from Lancaster in 1850.
Many of the residents earned their livelihood
making Bigelow carpets, hoop skirts, quilts,
combs, and counterpanes.

J.W. Barber made this sketch of Webster in 1839. The town was named for the famous statesman/orator. The lake on which Webster is located is rather long, and its original Indian name even longer — and almost impossible to pronounce.

The Joslin House was the place to stay in Webster in 1884. The town in its formative years had a tannery, a bleaching factory, and a plant for making thread.

In 1801, Southbridge was separated from nearby Sturbridge, although only 90 persons were involved in the newer town. By 1880 Southbridge had almost 6,000 residents, two hotels, nine schools, two banks, a public library, and a newspaper, plus manufactories turning out cotton goods, boots, shoes, and cutlery.

Sturbridge, next door to Southbridge, claimed such assets as good fish ponds in 1839, as well as six cotton mills, and mills for the production of wagons, sleighs, trunks, cigars, and chairs. Its founders would be surprised to see its fine recreated farming village.

Brookfield, in the southwestern part of Worcester county, was settled in 1660 by several families from Ipswich. The small town suffered ''exceedingly'' from raids in 1675 led by the Indian King Philip, and his Wampanoag tribesmen.

This Congregational Church was built at Brookfield in 1794. In the 1870's, one chronicler reported that the people of the town were industrious and frugal. They supported four churches, one hotel, and factories making bricks, ironware, carriages, and boots and shoes.

SNIPPET
Like most Massachusetts towns, Winchendon was quick to build churches, public schools, and libraries. In 1752 Winchendon had only ten families, but a church was organized in December of that same year. In the 1800's, the men and women of the town produced 898,000 pails, and 171,500 tubs in one year.

To the north of Worcester, towns like Leominster and Fitchburg came to life in the 18th century. Leominster, sketched here by J.W. Barber, was separated from Lancaster in 1740, and by 1840 had a population of 2,000. The big industry here was the manufacture of combs, with seventeen firms making $81,000 of combs per year, employing a total of 84 men and 47 women.

This southern view displays the town of Turkey Hills, eventually known as Fitchburg, which was described as large and flourishing in 1839. That same flattering phrase appears again in a Gazetteer of 1873, when Fitchburg had grown to 11,000 residents.

An 1867 Fitchburg advertisement offered equipment for paper mills. No less than seven such mills were operating in Fitchburg at that time. Among the other thriving industries: lumbering, and the manufacture of rattan furniture and fire engines.

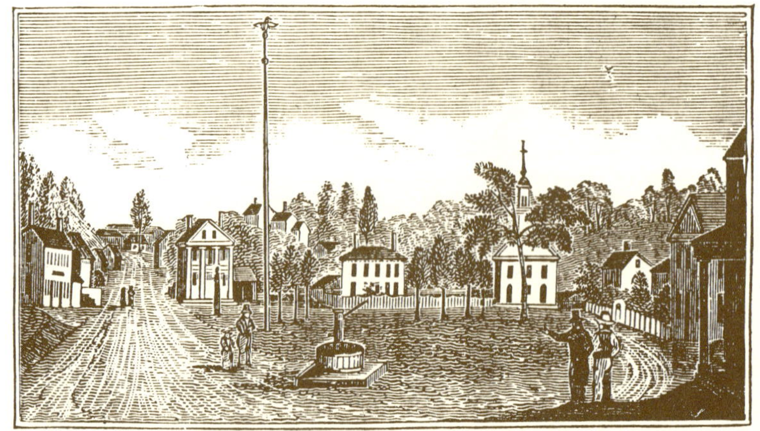

Athol, in the northwestern part of Worcester county, was settled in the 1730's, but growth was slow at first because of the danger of Indian raids. Athol is located on the Miller River, so named because a man named Miller drowned in it. In the 1870's, Athol claimed seventeen sawmills, and factories turning out palm-leaf hats, scythes, and shoe pegs.

In 1853, a tersely-worded Gazetteer describes the town of Barre as ''Surface elevated. Soil good. A busy town of miscellaneous manufacturers.'' That author might have added that Barre was a fine source of beef, pork, butter, and cheese, with three textile plants, and a factory which made axes.

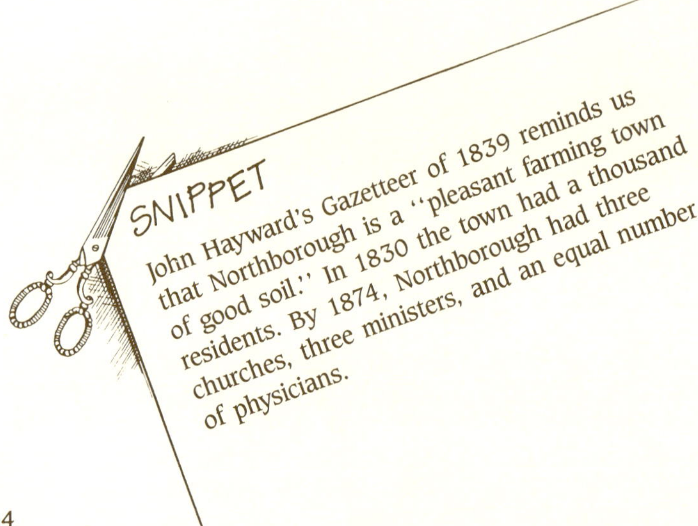

SNIPPET

John Hayward's Gazetteer of 1839 reminds us that Northborough is a ''pleasant farming town of good soil.'' In 1830 the town had a thousand residents. By 1874, Northborough had three churches, three ministers, and an equal number of physicians.

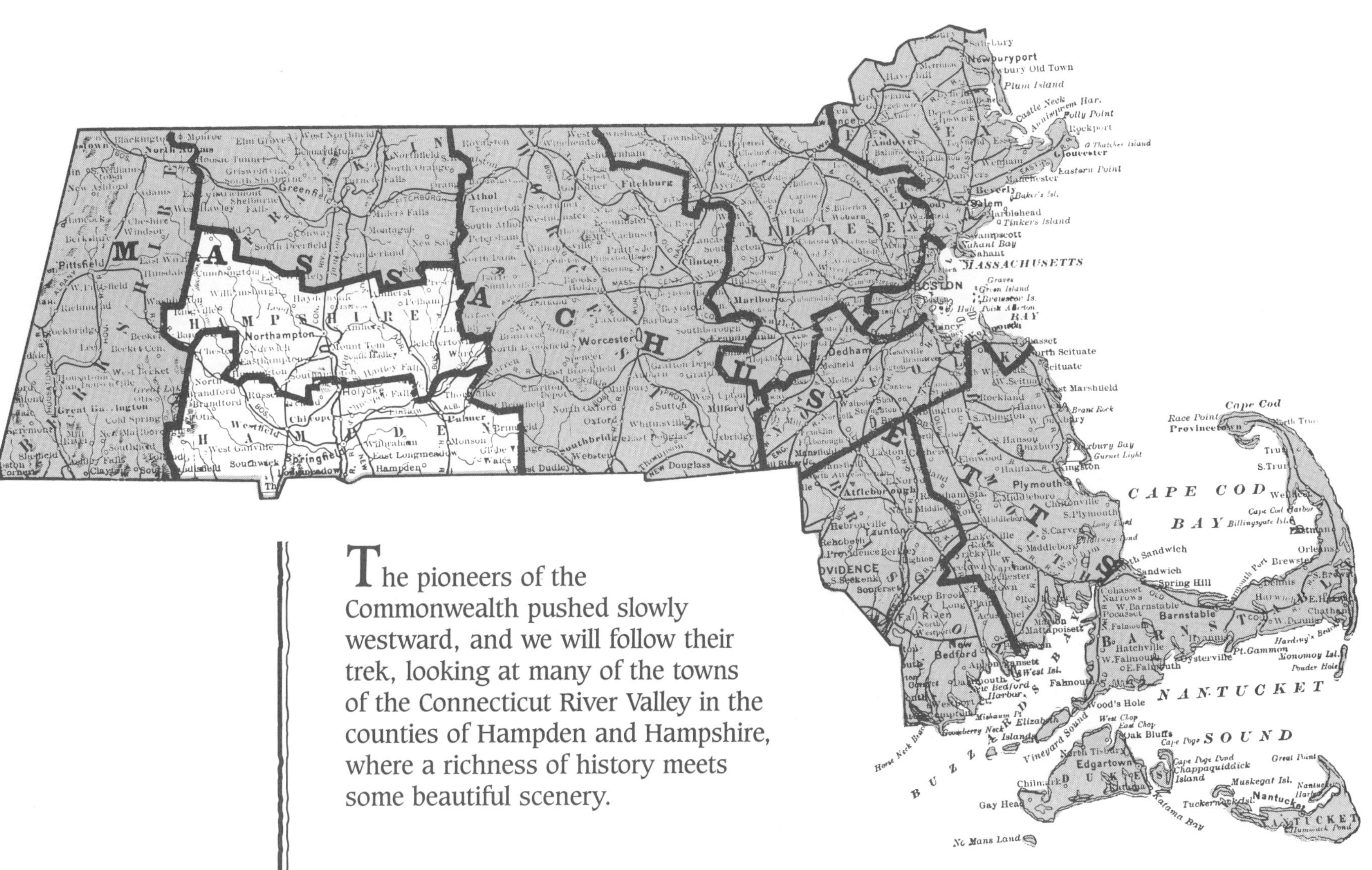

The pioneers of the Commonwealth pushed slowly westward, and we will follow their trek, looking at many of the towns of the Connecticut River Valley in the counties of Hampden and Hampshire, where a richness of history meets some beautiful scenery.

HAMPDEN & HAMPSHIRE
C O U N T I E S

The Connecticut River winds its way through Springfield, the chief city of Hampden County, in this sketch made in the 1870's. Springfield was settled in 1635, before Worcester, and was originally called Agawam.

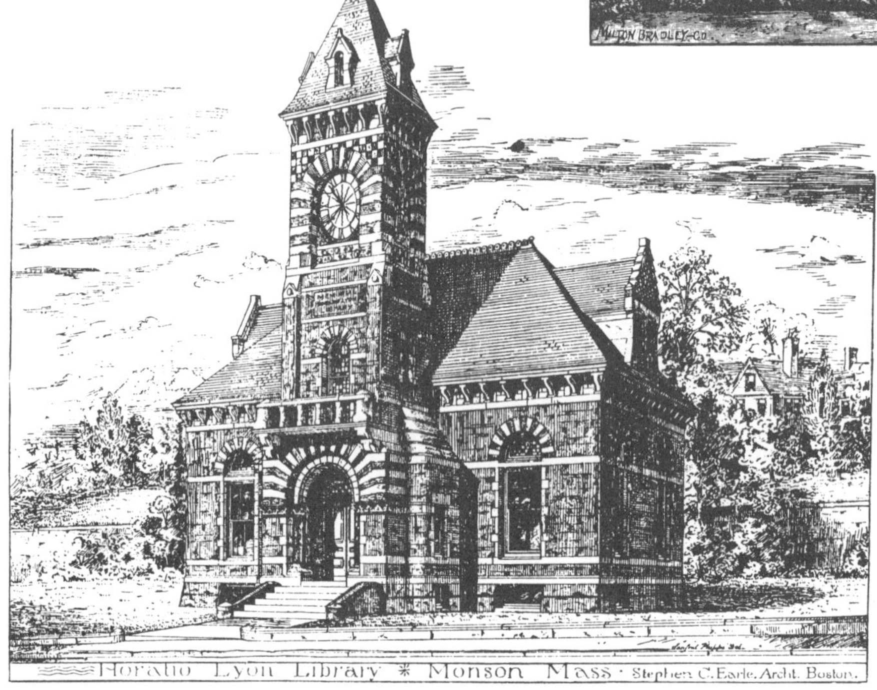

A few miles east of Springfield lies Monson, which was settled by 49 families in 1715. The town could claim this handsome library, a granite quarry, eleven public schools, and an academy by the 1870's. Its total assets include the nearby mountain views and "a scene of beautiful perspective."

Wilbraham, just east of Springfield, was incorporated in 1763, and its prominent Wesleyan Academy, pictured here, was incorporated in 1824. Wrote historian Elias Nason in the 1870's, "the scenery is remarkably beautiful, the land spreading out into winding glades and valleys."

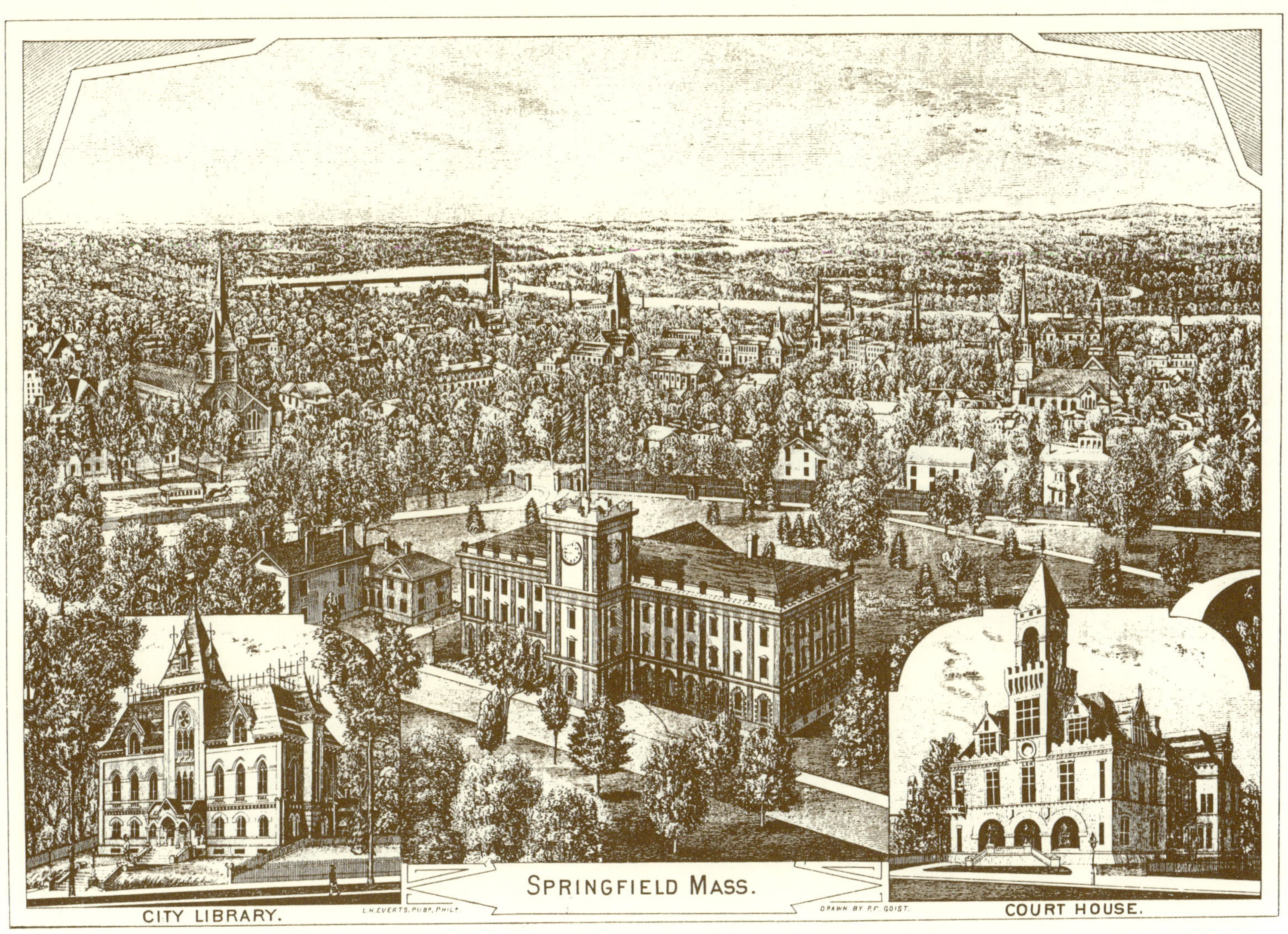

This 19th century drawing of Springfield shows the Armory at the center, with insets of the city library and court house — all built to last.

SNIPPET

Palmer was settled by a colony from Ireland in 1727. By 1874, the growing town had 3,631 inhabitants, three cotton mills, four sawmills, a newspaper, a savings bank, and 460 milch cows.

In the early years of the nation, a man named Daniel Shays led a revolt against high court fees, lawsuits, and against the powers of the Federal government, culminating in efforts to keep the courts from functioning in Springfield. The rebellion was quelled, with help from Governor Bowdoin.

The Smith and Wesson revolver factory moved to Springfield in 1856, and in 1880 Scientific American magazine showed us the factory and some of its workers.

Daniel B. Wesson employed 500 people in his revolver factory, and used a fine grade of steel with the stocks. His partner, inventor Horace Smith, retired in 1874, but Mr. Wesson kept plugging away until his death in 1906.

Another leading citizen of Springfield was Samuel Bowles, born in 1826. He founded the ''Springfield Republican'' newspaper, and was an able historian and author of several books.

109

George Washington authorized the Armory in 1795, and in 1852 Harper's Monthly magazine sketched "the new arsenal" at Springfield shown here. In its three-story building, we are told, could be stored no less than 300,000 muskets.

The "proving house" at the Springfield Armory was used to test loaded gun barrels, the huge timbers reinforced as a protection against misfires or fires.

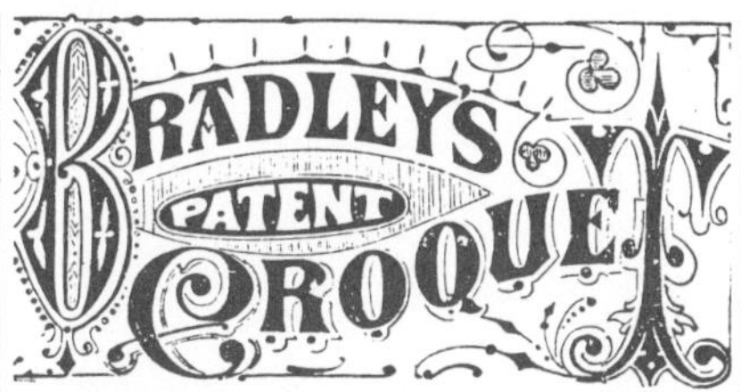

THE PATENT SOCKET BRIDGE.

Look on this picture then on THAT

THE ORDINARY BRIDGE

After one day's playing.

PROF. ROVER'S

Manual of Croquet,

The standard authority in America. Price, only 10 cents. With new design for setting a ground. Send stamp for complete Catalogue of Games.

MILTON, BRADLEY & CO.,

Springfield, Mass.

Two well-known names from Springfield appeared in a directory of New England manufacturers in 1867 — one for avid readers, and the other for lovers of lawn sports with a minimum of violence.

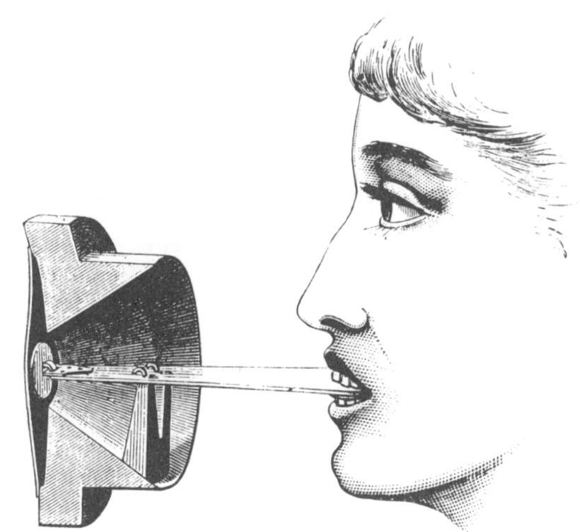

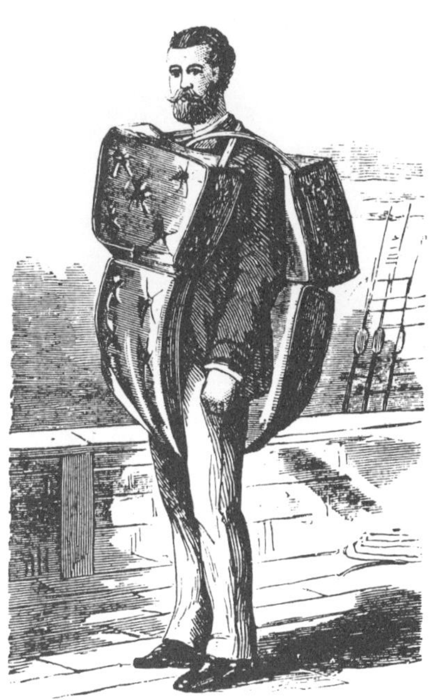

Scientific American magazine took note of the patented inventiveness of two of Springfield's residents. In 1875, Mr. J.F. Peck thought the world might welcome his new life-preserving mattress, while in 1880 Mr. H.G. Fiske suggested a dental attachment for telephones to aid the hard-of-hearing.

Springfield's better inns in the 1870's included the Massasoit House and Cooley's, as displayed in these old advertisements. At that time, a historian praised the city, its industry, and its beauty, but added that "the city is in need of a good water supply and a good local history."

West Springfield, along the west bank of the Connecticut River, was part of Springfield until its incorporation in 1773. Mr. Barber described this scene as an ancient church of West Springfield, adding that the first organized church was formed here in 1698.

Chicopee, like the river of the same name, has a history of many spellings, including Chickopee, Chicapee, and Chickabee. Formerly the northern part of Springfield, the city was the home of that pioneering automobile, the Stevens-Duryea, while the Knox car was manufactured in nearby Springfield.

THE STEVENS-DURYEA.

THE 1904 KNOX.

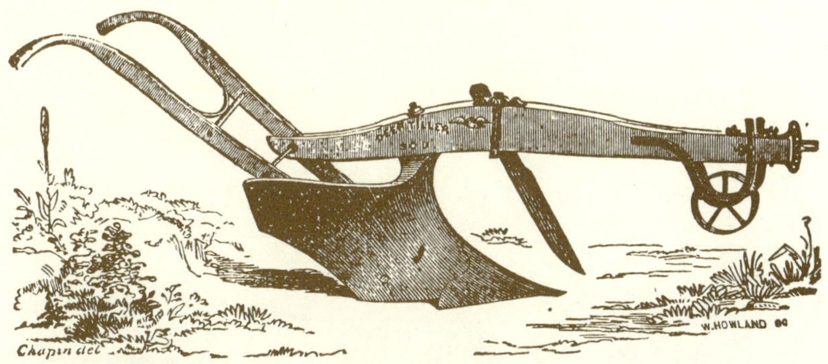

In Chicopee Falls, the Whittemore and Belcher firm sold all sorts of agricultural tools, while the farms of the area grew Indian corn, broom corn, rye, buckwheat, oats, hay, and exactly 16,176 apple trees. No count of apples was provided.

SNIPPET

Edward Bellamy, the well-known author of "Looking Backward," was born in Chicopee Falls in 1850.

Westfield, a few miles from Springfield, was proud of its state normal school, which had 162 pupils in 1872, and was ''for gentlemen as well as ladies.'' In 1837, Westfield had three thousand residents, one third of whom were involved in the manufacture of buggy whips.

The Crane brothers, makers of fine papers, moved from Ballston Spa, N.Y. to Westfield in 1869, and when their plant burned down the following year, built this fine brick structure, where 75 employees made two tons of paper each day.

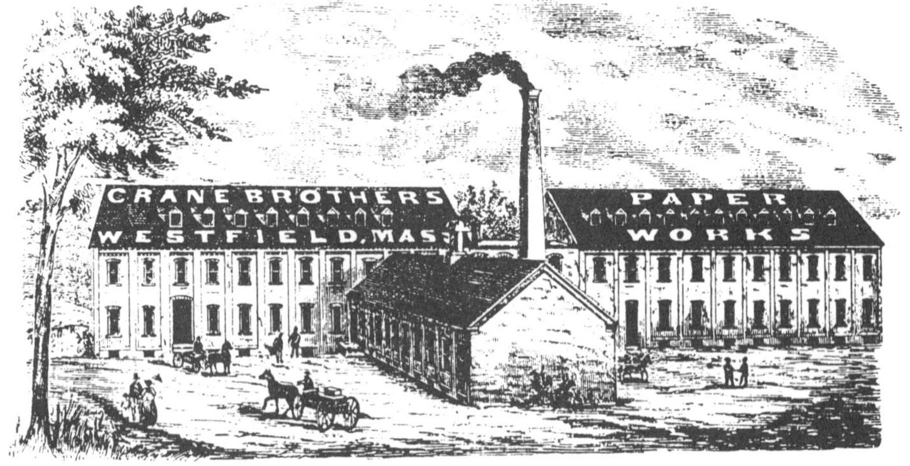

Holyoke is another Massachusetts city which
emerged as an inland center of growth in the
19th century. The Holyoke town hall, shown
here, was built of granite only a few years
after the city was incorporated, and
was described as one of the finest
such buildings in the state.

SNIPPET

Once a part of Springfield,
Ludlow was incorporated in
1774, and the first church
was organized in 1789.
Pastor Stewart was paid a
yearly salary of $200 and
thirty cords of wood.

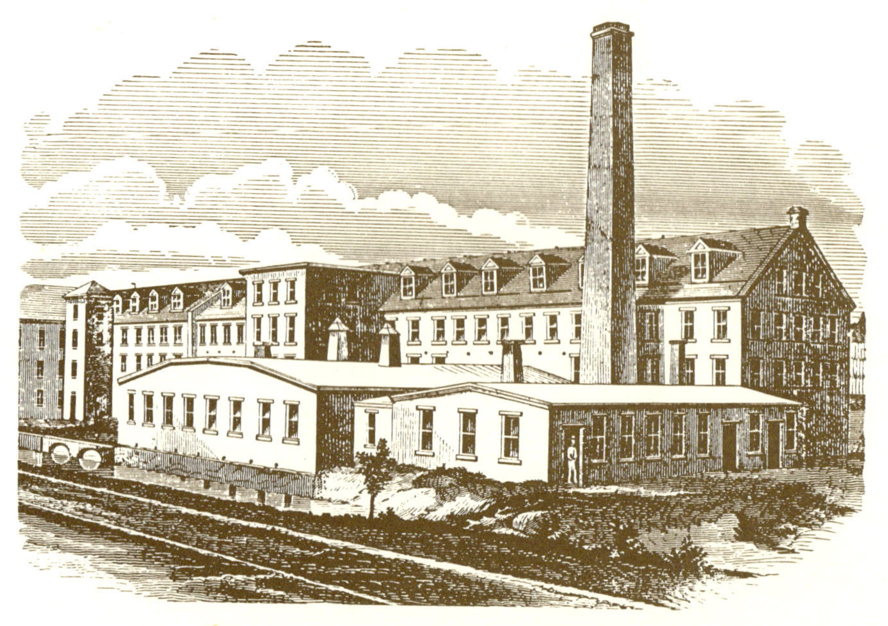

By the 1870's, Holyoke had fourteen paper mills, including the Holyoke Paper Company, shown here. Together, the paper mills provided employment for more than 2,000 men and women.

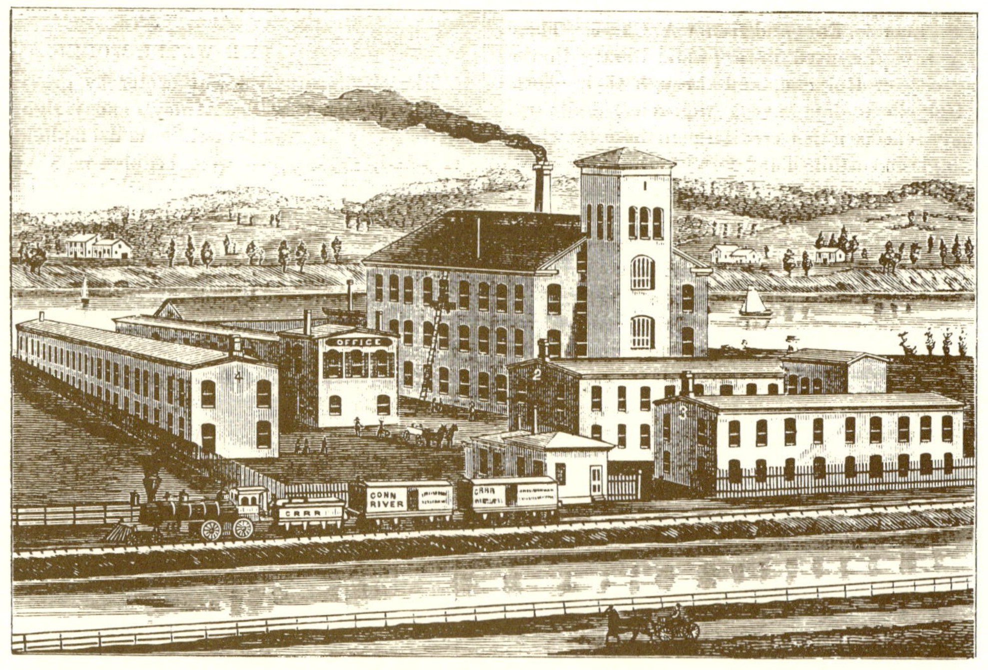

The Springfield Blanket Company was organized in 1870, and in this Holyoke plant manufactured 125,000 horse blankets a year — one of the many diversified industries of the city.

Thanks to a Scientific American magazine of 1880, we can look inside the Albion Paper Company at Holyoke, where women were sorting rags to be used in the manufacture of top grade paper for books.

William Whiting was one of Holyoke's most successful citizens, serving as mayor, owner of several paper mills and the Windsor Hotel, shown here.

The Holyoke opera house, as sketched about 1880, was built as a community asset by William Whiting. It was described by one impartial observer as one of the most handsome in the country, and ''complete in all its appointments.''

The town of Ware, in southeast Hampshire county, sketched here by J.W. Barber, received rather harsh treatment from Dr. Dwight, the historian, who called the soil ''inferior.'' A second historian, Elias Nason, erroneously placed the town in the southwestern part of the county.

Mr. C.A. Stevens, pictured here, was a textile pioneer in Ware, building a mill for the manufacture of broadcloth in the 1840's, and in 1870 building the ''Ware Opera House.'' That name had no musical significance, but the mill made ''opera flannel'' cloth. The town at that time had some 4,200 residents.

SNIPPET

In 1796, Rev. Mix visited Rev. Stoddard and his wife and four daughters in Northampton to find a wife. After introductions, he asked for the hand of eldest daughter Mary, saying that he would smoke his pipe in an adjoining room while she considered the offer. Mary said she needed more time, and he left, but he received a letter a few weeks later, as follows: ''Dear Mr. Mix: Yes (signed) Mary Stoddard.'' The writer reported that the couple had a fine happy marriage.

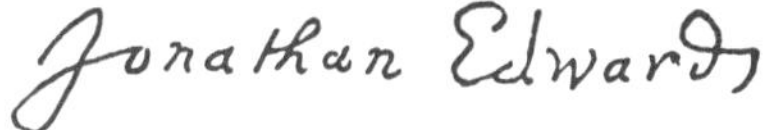

Northampton, the chief town of Hampshire County, was settled in 1654, on the west bank of the Connecticut River. This 19th century view shows the courthouse and one of the three Congregational churches in the central part of town.

Jonathon Edwards' long ministry in Northampton was marked by a religious revival which won him national notice. He asserted that the people of Hampshire County were sober, orderly, and as good as any in New England. He was installed as President of Princeton in 1758, and died of smallpox only a month later.

Timothy Dwight, born in Northampton in 1752, was President of Yale from 1795 to 1817. Among his many writings is the four volume work entitled ''Travels in New England.'' He was an ardent advocate of higher education for women.

The business of the town of Northampton was
initially conducted in a modest ''meeting-house,''
and in 1823 in a small courthouse. The ''new''
courthouse shown here was erected in 1851.

SNIPPET

Thoreau, writing in 1840, wrote that ''the first
settlers made preparations to drink a good deal,
and did not disappoint themselves.''

Visitors to the Northampton scene of 1830 might have some difficulty in deciding whether this handsome building was a seminary, courthouse, library, or other public building. It was actually the residence of Mr. Joseph Bowers, whose career is not mentioned in several history books, but who apparently earned an ''A'' for affluence.

Smith College was dedicated in Northampton in 1875, with Professor Seelye of nearby Amherst as President. This 1894 drawing shows a ''white-robed'' commencement ceremony. The college, whose origins reflect the generosity of Sophia Smith of Hatfield, soon earned the prestige already established at Amherst and Williams.

South Hadley shares the beautiful setting of many towns of the Connecticut River valley, and like Northampton, had and has a special asset in the form of Mt. Holyoke College. When it opened its doors in 1837, it was called Mt. Holyoke Seminary. This view was sketched about 1880.

Mount Tom appears across the Connecticut River from South Hadley. This drawing of 1880 added a credit line saying ''after a sketch from Mr. Bartlett'' — no doubt a borrowing from the great engraver of that name.

Easthampton was originally a part of Northampton, but was incorporated as a town in 1809. This old engraving shows us Williston Seminary, which opened its doors in 1841 as a preparatory school for young men and women. The ''female department'' was suspended in 1864.

There were 316,000 students taught by 9,200 teachers in the public schools of the state in 1875. The average school year was eight months and seventeen days.

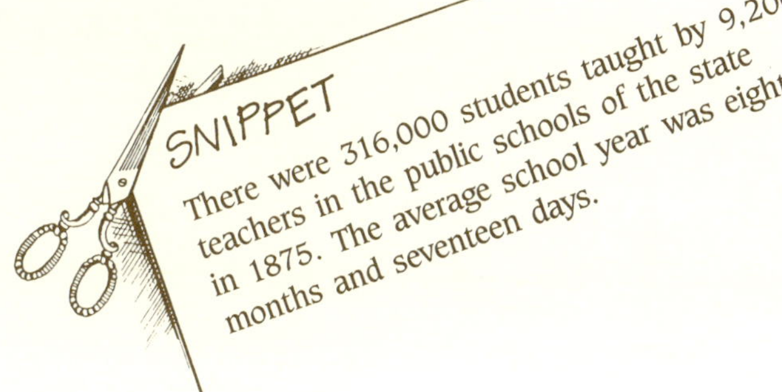

Edmund Sawyer, shown here, was a business associate of Mr. Williston, a director of three textile firms and two banks, a trustee of Mt. Holyoke, Williston Seminary, and a Northampton Hospital, a state senator, and a man whose financial acumen was a considerable asset for the community.

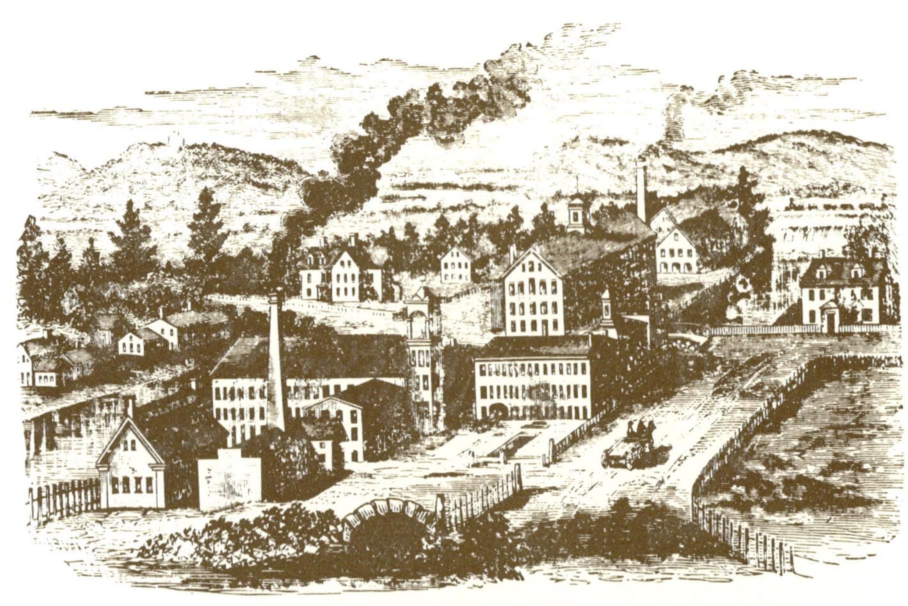

Florence, the small town neighbor of Northampton, was the 19th century home of the Nonotuck Silk Company, one of the largest silk goods manufacturers in the country in the 1870's, when this drawing appeared.

Amherst College, as it looked in 1848. The academy of the same name opened its doors in 1814, and the college seven years later, soon acquiring a reputation of excellence.

Amherst was also the home of the Massachusetts College of Agriculture, founded in 1863, with a graduating class of thirteen young men in 1873. The town itself, back in 1783, had five taverners and eight rum sellers, along with two temperance societies.

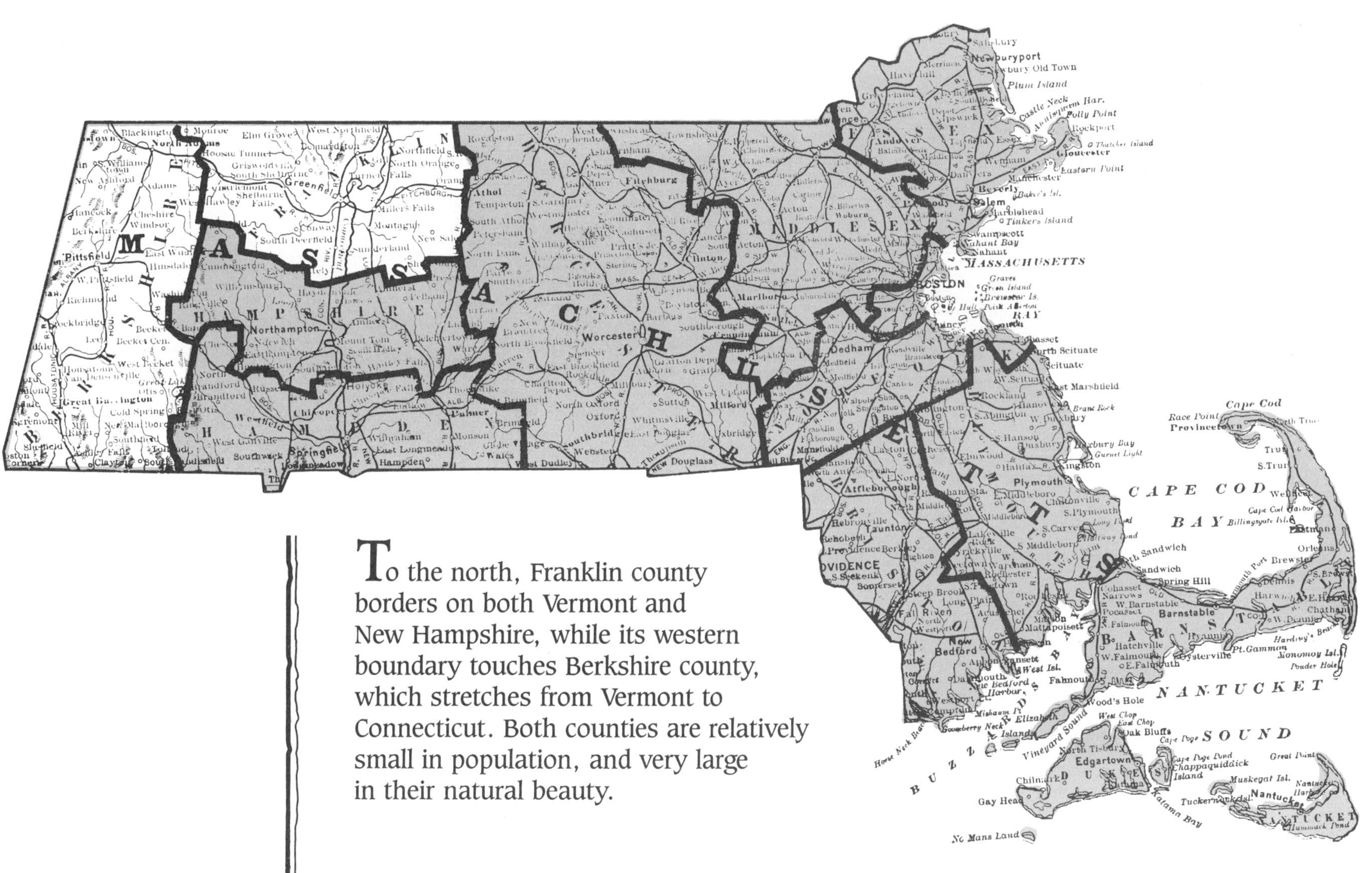

To the north, Franklin county borders on both Vermont and New Hampshire, while its western boundary touches Berkshire county, which stretches from Vermont to Connecticut. Both counties are relatively small in population, and very large in their natural beauty.

FRANKLIN & BERKSHIRE
COUNTIES

Deerfield, in Franklin County, suffered the loss of seventy young men in an Indian ambush in 1675, but its long-range history is based in a setting of rare beauty. This is Deerfield in 1839, along the west bank of the Connecticut River.

SNIPPET

Among the many colonial church rules was one which counseled that speaking ill of the minister would incur severe punishment, while another warned that those singing or dancing vainly were admonished to cease. During church services, officers with long wands were appointed to correct slumberers who were not listening to sermons.

J.W. Barber sketched this ancient ''Indian House'' in 1839 — one of the buildings which escaped the Indian raids, and stood until 1848. Deerfield has preserved many of its older homes, as well as its charm.

Deerfield Academy was dedicated in 1799, and
in its first year enrolled 292 students from four
different towns. This is a newer Deerfield
building, opened in 1879, through the generosity
of the Dickinson family. The school has
maintained its reputation for excellence all
of these years.

Turners Falls, on the Connecticut River near Greenfield, is shown here. The village was not founded until 1867, but soon thereafter could claim two paper mills, a lumber company, and a cutlery firm which employed 600 people. By 1879 the village had 2,000 residents.

This is Mr. Barber's drawing of Greenfield, the county seat, as it appeared in 1839. The spire at the left belongs to the courthouse, while the spire at the right is atop the Congregational Church.

John Russell's large plant near Greenfield made the finest cutlery in the nation, according to Albert Bolles, a writer and economist of 1889. The town of Greenfield was incorporated in 1853.

In the 1800's, the town of Orange was described as a "sprightly farming and manufacturing" place, whose people made palm-leaf hats, shoe pegs, and sewing machines.

The Mansion House was a popular Greenfield hotel when this sketch appeared about 1879. Forty years earlier, the town had 1,840 residents, many of whom produced lead pipes, rifles, pistols, trunks, leather goods, and tinware. An academy for young women and a farm school for young men provided educational strength for the town.

Northfield, whose main street is pictured here, was purchased from the Indians in 1687. Sitting on the east side of the Connecticut River, near the New Hampshire border, the town is described by an author of 1853 as "a scene of rare beauty and repose." Visitors of today might have similar sentiments about Northfield.

Tucked away in the northwest corner of Berkshire County are Adams and North Adams, this being an 1839 view of the northern village. Both villages were subject to Indian attacks in the years from 1746 to 1756.

The underground removal of rock from one tunnel shaft is shown here. Several construction workers lost their lives before the tunnel was finished, but the completion brought new growth, fame, and prosperity for the North Adams area in the 1870's.

The building of a tunnel through Hoosac mountain to provide rail service from Troy, N.Y. to North Adams was a huge engineering feat which got under way in 1855. This sketch, from the first issue of Scribner's Monthly magazine, shows a construction crew about to descend to the central tunnel shaft.

Susan B. Anthony was born in Adams in 1820, and was a strong leader in the anti-slavery movement. With Elizabeth Cady Stanton, she led the forces working for women's suffrage, and for their rights to higher education.

Williamstown, a few miles from North Adams, was incorporated in 1765, and named for Col. Ephraim Williams, as was the college of the same name. This 1839 view shows some of its buildings. Williams was incorporated in 1793, and the beauty of the town and the reputation of the college seem secure.

This old sketch by Harry Fenn shows Mount Greylock from a spot near Williamstown. The mountain is the highest in Massachusetts, with an altitude of 3,505 feet.

Mr. Barber sketched the central part of Pittsfield in 1839, as viewed from the west. The largest city in Berkshire County, Pittsfield was originally called ''Boston Plantation.'' The town had only twenty cabins in 1758, but was incorporated just three years later. The park area in the center, borrowing from Boston, was the ''Common.''

This 1879 drawing shows Pittsfield's railroad depot — a busy terminal for the Boston and Albany, the Housatonic and Pittsfield, and the North Adams rail lines.

Justice was meted out at the Pittsfield courthouse – this drawing by Milton Bradley. In 1874, we are advised, the growing city could boast two banks, two newspapers, a library, jail, and many elegant churches and residences.

Herman Melville, born in 1819, lived in Pittsfield for some time, and although it took many years for him to gain proper recognition, he was finally recognized for his writings about the sea, and his masterful ''Moby Dick.''

Lenox, on the Housatonic River south of Pittsfield, had 1,177 residents in 1839. Here we see the Townhouse at the right, and Wilson's three-story hotel next to it.

An 1894 sketch by W.S. Vanderbilt Allen
shows us the summer scene at Lenox, with this
drive around a nearby lake...a popular resort
area, then and now.

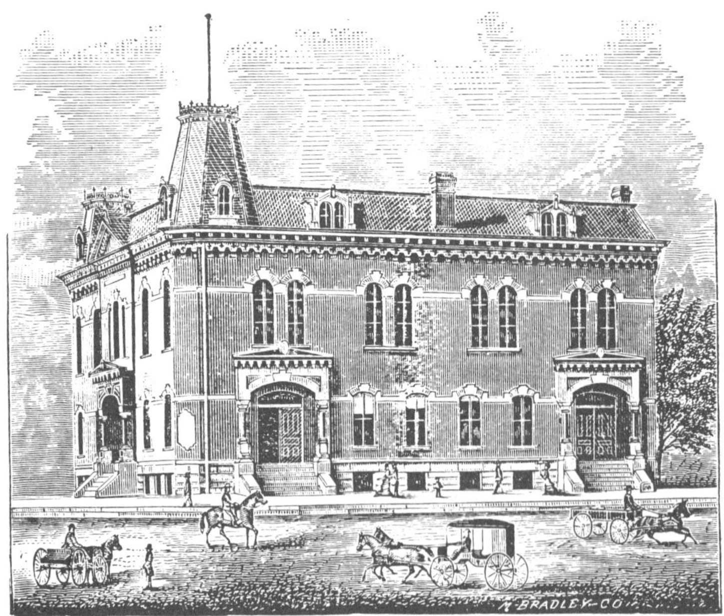

In the 19th century, the town of Lee remembered its men who served in the Civil War with this Memorial Hall, costing all of $29,000, and containing a public library as well as the town offices. At one time, the town had ten paper mills in operation.

In 1839, J.W. Barber sketched the oldest home in Stockbridge, another one of the pretty towns of the Berkshires. The house was built in 1737, and was the home of Rev. Jonathon Edwards for some time. One historian in 1874 described the place in simple but meaningful terms as ''a very beautiful town. . .168 miles from Boston.''

William Cullen Bryant was born in Cummington, but spent many happy years in Great Barrington, sharing this home with the owner, and paying him all of thirty dollars a year. Bryant and the people of Great Barrington shared a great affection for the town and for each other.

Bryant was happy to receive a fee of two dollars for some of the many poems he wrote, and even happier to meet and marry Fanny Fairchild. As one writer noted, Fanny "was for forty-five years the stay and blessing of his life." This is the home at Great Barrington in which Bryant and Miss Fairchild were married.

''By the sword we seek peace,
But peace only under liberty.''

ACKNOWLEDGEMENTS

My thanks for the help provided by so many writers and artists who are memories from another era. The bibliography for ''Picture Book of Old Massachusetts'' cannot do justice to all of those who have recorded the proud history of Massachusetts, but this is a belated note of gratitude to such writers and artists as Elias Nason, Benson Lossing, George Austin, Moses King, Samuel Adams Drake, John Hayward, Samuel Goodrich, William Swinton, and many others.

In honoring these names of long ago, I should pay particular tribute to the memory of John Warner Barber, Jedidiah Morse, and W.H. Bartlett, whose works are already treasured by bookmen everywhere.

To the descendants of those outstanding magazines of the 19th century, our thanks as well to Century, Scientific American, Harper's Monthly, Scribner's Monthly and Scribner's Magazine, for their early contributions to the history of the Bay State.

More recently, our thanks to Dover Publications for use of illustrations from Mr. Gillon's fine book about American architecture, and a special acknowledgement for the help of Mrs. Barrows Mussey, whose late husband inspired my great respect for the role of the great writers, artists, and engravers of New England in the 1800's. The 20th century writings of Barrows Mussey remain as proof positive that history is seldom dull, and neither should the telling of it be so.

The preparation of ''Picture Book of Old Massachusetts'' deserves editing thanks for Pewilla Dick, and great gratitude to Gretchen and Susan. Gretchen is Gretchen Bradley, whose first book design work for me was the earlier companion piece called ''Picture Book of Old Connecticut.'' My five-star thanks also go to Susan Duncan, who is not only my partner, but a proofreader with wonderful patience, and a belief that perhaps the reader might forgive a slight slip-up.

Sam Tuttle

BIBLIOGRAPHY

Pictoral Description of the United States, Robert Sears, 1848

Gazetteer of the state of Massachusetts, Elias Nason, 1874

Pictorial History of the United States,
  Benson J. Lossing, 1858

National History of the United States,
  Benson J. Lossing, 1855

History of Massachusetts, George L. Austin, 1876

Farmer's Almanack, Robert B. Thomas, 1843-1854

United States Textile Directory, John Hayes, 1875

King's Handbook of Boston, Moses King, 1878

Perley's Reminiscences, Perley Poore, 1886

Annual Report, U.S. Commerce and Navigation,
  James Guthrie, 1855

Hayward's United States Gazetteer, John Hayward, 1851

History of the United States, Samuel Goodrich, 1842

Old Landmarks and Historic Personages of Boston,
  Samuel Adams Drake, 1900

A Book of American Explorers, Thomas W. Higginson, 1877

King's Dictionary of Boston, Edwin M. Bacon, 1883

Compendium, Seventh Census of the U.S.,
  J.D.B. DeBow, 1854

The American Gazetteer, Jedidiah Morse, 1804

Historical Collections: Massachusetts,
  John Warner Barber, 1839

Centennial Gazetteer of the United States,
  A. von Steinwehr, 1874

Annual Report, U.S. Commerce and Navigation,
  Edward Young, 1875

Old New England, Barrows Mussey, 1946

Geography Made Easy, Jedidiah Morse, 1814

One Hundred Years' Progress of the United States,
  L. Stebbins, 1870

The Critical Period of American History, John Fiske, 1888

Condensed United States History, William Swinton, 1871

Spectacles for Young Eyes, S.W. Lander, 1863

The Making of New England, Samuel Adams Drake, 1894

Nooks and Corners of the New England Coast,
  Samuel Adams Drake, 1875

Geographical, Historical, and Commercial Grammar and
  Present State of the Several Kingdoms of the World,
  William Guthrie, 1790

Peculiarities of American Cities, William Glazier, 1886

Early Illustrations and Views of American Architecture,
  Edmund V. Gillon, Jr., 1971

History of the Connecticut Valley in Massachusetts,
  Vol. 1 & 2, Louis H. Everts, 1879

The People's Family Atlas of the World,
  People's Publishing Co., 1884

Selected issues of Century, Harper's Monthly,
  Scribner's Monthly, Scribner's Magazine, and
  Scientific American 19th century editions

Selected 19th century editions of New England
  Business Directory and Boston Directory

Triumphs of Enterprise, Ingenuity, and Public Spirit,
  James Parton, 1872

Merry's Museum, Samuel G. Goodrich, 1842

Appleton's Northern and Eastern Traveler's Guide,
  W. Williams, 1851

Industrial History of the United States, A.S. Bolles, 1889

Our First Century, R.M. Devens, 1880

Eminent American Mechanics, Henry Howe, 1844

Great Industries of the United States,
  Horace Greeley, 1892

New System of Geography, Jedidiah Morse, 1822

Universal Gazetteer, Jedidiah Morse, 1821

INDEX OF PLACES